J
796.41
D
Dolan, Edward F   1924-
    The complete beginner's guide to gym-
nastics / Edward F. Dolan, Jr. ; with
photos. by James Stewart. -- 1st ed. --
Garden City, N.Y. : Doubleday, 1980.
   209p. ill.
(The Complete beginner's guide series)

    SUMMARY: An introduction to gymnas-
tics describing the basic exercises,
equipment, and the eight competitive
events and the more than 100 stunts
that can be performed in them.
    ISBN 0-385-13434-7 : $8.95. ISBN 0-

1. Gymnastics.   bfc 6 and up

                                          55390
                              78-60286 Je80
                              CIP MARC AC

The Complete Beginner's Guide to Gymnastics

The Complete Beginner's Guide to Gymnastics

EDWARD F. DOLAN, JR.

With Photographs by James Stewart

Doubleday & Company, Inc.   Garden City, New York   1980

Library of Congress Cataloging in Publication Data

Dolan, Edward F   1924–
The complete beginner's guide to gymnastics.

(The complete beginner's guide series)
Includes index.
SUMMARY: An introduction to gymnastics describing the basic exercises, equipment, and the eight competitive events and the more than 100 stunts that can be performed in them.
1. Gymnastics—Juvenile literature.   [1. Gymnastics]
I. Stewart, James, 1909–   II. Title.
GV461.D64   796.4'1
ISBN: 0-385-13434-7 Trade
        0-385-13435-5 Prebound
Library of Congress Catalog Card Number 78–60286

This book is for Tracy and Melanie,
two goods friends in Africa

I am indebted to many people for their help in the preparation of this book. First, for the photographic use of their facilities, my thanks must go to the City Recreation Department of San Rafael, California (and especially to Jim Carr and Susan Martin); to Gymmarin of San Rafael; and to the Steve Hug School of Gymnastics, San Rafael.

Special thanks are due to gymnasts Kerry Bray, Karen Evering, Valerie Johnson, Colleen Keating, Maureen Keating, Sheila Northern, Brad Steffen, and Stephanie Yahata for all their fine work.

Particular thanks are due to gymnasts Lyn Kaveney and two-time Olympian Steve Hug. Both worked tirelessly. Steve, who appeared in the 1968 Olympics at Mexico City and the 1972 Olympics at Munich, not only performed for our camera but also made some good suggestions for the book.

Contents

The Complete Beginner's Guide to Gymnastics

Welcome to Gymnastics

Gymnastics is a sport that's at least five thousand years old. As far as anyone can tell, it began in Egypt. Later, it was practiced in ancient China, India, Greece, and Rome. Then, following the fall of the Roman Empire, it was forgotten by all but a few devotees for centuries to come.

But today, this ancient sport is enjoying a new popularity, thanks to the talents of such Olympians as Olga Korbut, Nadia Comaneci, Nelli Kim, Kathy Rigby, and Bart Connor. And let's not forget the courage of Japan's Shun Fujimoto, who won a medal on the rings in the 1976 Olympics and then collapsed because he had been performing with a broken kneecap. Their exploits have captivated television viewers all across the world.

And—more important—their skills and daring have encouraged countless young people to try the sport for themselves. Some have come to gymnastics just for the sheer fun of it. And some with the idea of seeing just how far they can go in competition—perhaps right to some future Olympics.

Today's young gymnasts find themselves in a sport far different from the one practiced in ancient times. In its early days, the games and exercises were mainly of the sort intended to develop combative skills that soldiers could use in battle. And in Greece—the country that gave us the word *gymnastics*—the exercises were all done in the nude. The word orginally meant "naked art."

Gymnastics as we know it today can be traced back to the early nineteenth century and to men such as Pehr Ling of Sweden and Friedrich Jahn of Germany. Realizing that the almost-forgotten sport was an excellent builder of the body and spirit, they established schools for its practice. Of the two, Jahn is the one remembered today. His ideas on training spread throughout the world. He invented much of the equipment now used. In time, Jahn won the title "the father of modern gymnastics."

There are many different activities in modern gymnastics. They range from the trampoline, rope climbing, and juggling with Indian clubs to the parallel bars and vaulting. But of all the activities available, eight receive the most attention. They are the ones that are classed as competitive events.

These eight competitive events are divided into six for men and four for women. In case your eyebrows just went up at this strange arithmetic, it can be accounted for the fact that two of the events are open to both men and women.

Here is the way the eight are divided:

Men	*Women*
Floor exercise	Floor exercise
Vaulting	Vaulting
Rings	Balance beam
Side horse	Uneven parallel bars
Parallel bars	
Horizontal bar	

In the main, the events are divided between the men and the women along the lines of strength. Those demanding the greatest strength go to the men. While strength also plays a part in women's events (make no mistake about that!), the accent is put more on grace and suppleness.

And what of all the activities that are not competitive events—the trampoline, rope climbing, Indian clubs, and such? Often, they're taught in school or in a local recreation program, and so you'll likely have many a chance to enjoy them if you wish. As for the trampoline, it's been developed into a sport of its own.

This book, however, will concentrate on the eight competitive events, presenting more than a hundred stunts that can be performed in them. We'll start with everyone together, first with a chapter on basic exercises that will serve you well in any event, and then with one on floor exercise.

Next, we'll work on two women's events—the balance beam and the uneven parallel bars. Then it's on to chapters for the men, one each on the rings, side horse, parallel bars, and horizontal bar. Finally, we'll all get together again, this time for a chapter on vaulting.

A word has to be said here about the kinds of stunts you'll find in the coming pages. There are three general levels in gymnastics training—beginning, intermediate, and advanced. Just as the title says, this is a book for beginners, and so most of the stunts will be beginning ones. But there will be some intermediate ones sprinkled throughout to add to the fun and challenge.

And if you're planning to go just as far as you can in gymnastics, the closing chapter is especially for you. Called "A Look to the Future," it contains a series of the most popular advanced stunts—one for each event—and is meant to give you an idea of the exciting things you'll one day be doing.

The chapters will see us working on various pieces of equipment. Each piece of equipment will be described as we come to it. But so that you'll know what to expect, here now is a glimpse of the equipment.

You won't need a great deal of personal gear to begin your work. Leotards are worn by women, both in practice and competition. Men may practice in shorts or lightweight trousers and a T-shirt; for competition, the men will need to purchase a gymnastics outfit consisting of body shirt and white, tapered trousers. Everyone may wear gymnastics slippers or socks when practicing.

Gymnastics is one of the safest of sports. But there can be some pretty nasty falls from the equipment if you don't exercise a little common-sense care. And so, from the very moment that we begin work, please keep the following safety rules firmly in mind:

1. Use the equipment only for practice and performance. It's not there to be played on.
2. Check the equipment to see that it's in good working order—steady and secure—before ever getting up on it.

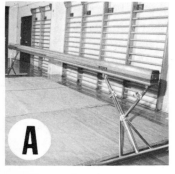

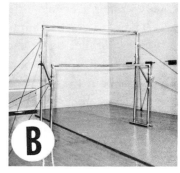

Gymnastics Equipment
Pictured are: (A) balance beam,
(B) uneven parallel bars, (C) rings,
(D) side horse, (E) parallel bars,
(F) horizontal bar, and (G) vaulting horse.

3. Always be sure that there are gym mats placed on the floor under and around the equipment.

4. Practice each new stunt down on or close to the floor before testing it on the equipment.

5. Always use one or more spotters when you take a stunt "aloft" for the first time. A spotter is an experienced gymnast—perhaps a friend, perhaps your coach—who stands below to advise you, to provide support against a fall, and to break the fall if you do tumble.

6. When working on the "bars" equipment, be sure to use gymnastics chalk (magnesium carbonate) on your hands. It will reduce perspiration and give you a firmer grip on the bar.

   Also, it may be wise to wear handguards as a protection against blistering and tearing. Glovelike and usually made of leather, they can be purchased quite inexpensively. Make sure that they fit properly so that they won't wrinkle and further chafe the hands.

   Many coaches feel that beginners should not wear the guards but should give their hands every chance to toughen.

   Between practice sessions, you can keep your hands soft with applications of hand lotion.

7. Always take a few minutes to "limber up" before beginning to practice. The accent should be on stretching exercises. Those few minutes can save you many a sore muscle—and many a clumsy slip from the equipment.

Gymnastics work will do many things for you. In particular, it will develop your strength, agility, flexibility, co-ordination, and stamina. To assist in that development, you'll be wise to work up a daily program of general exercise. It should put emphasis on those areas— perhaps your stamina, perhaps some slack abdominal muscles—that seem to need the most attention.

It will be a good idea to talk with your coach about all this (and, if you're seriously planning to compete, you really should try to find a coach as soon as you can). Knowing you well, the coach will be able to suggest the kinds of exercises that will best suit your individual needs.

Well, that's it. The time has come to work.

So welcome to gymnastics, and let's get started.

1 For Everyone– Getting Started

As every athlete knows, all work in any sport must begin with the fundamentals. In gymnastics, the fundamentals can be summed up in two words—*tumbling* and *balancing*.

TUMBLING AND BALANCING

You'll be using these two skills for as long as you're a gymnast. Tumbling will enable you to flow through all sorts of somersaults, cartwheels, walkovers, body twists, and handsprings; it will also give you the agility to handle all other gymnastic actions easily and gracefully. Balance, of course, will keep you from tottering, stumbling, or falling as you perform any movement, no matter how simple or complex it might be.

These two skills will be a must in whatever event you choose to enter. Each plays a vital role in floor exercise. Each is used on all pieces of equipment. For instance, as a woman, you'll need such tumbling stunts as the cartwheel and walkover for the balance beam. And you'll be constantly putting your balance to the test up there with pivots, supports, scales, and dance steps.

And if you're a man: You'll find that skin-the-cat on the rings is much the same as the simple backward roll in beginning tumbling. As for balance—well, ask any gymnast if you can work on the side horse or the parallel bars without it.

Training in tumbling and balancing can begin with nine simple exercises. They're fun to do and can be practiced on a gym mat at school or on any soft surface at home—perhaps a folded blanket or a patch of backyard lawn. No special clothing is needed. Sneakers and shorts or slacks will do fine. If you wish, you can work in your bare feet.

If you'll give these beginning exercises some dedicated practice, they should do many things for you. Out of them, first, should come a greater agility and flexibility, and a sharper sense of balance. Also, better co-ordination and muscular control. And a steadily growing confidence in your ability to make your body do what you command it to do. In all, the exercises should give you a solid start toward the day when you'll be mastering some of the most challenging movements in gymnastics.

So let's find a soft spot and get to work.

BASIC EXERCISES

Exercise 1: The Forward Roll

The forward roll is a very simple somersault. To get into the starting position (Picture A), squat down and place your hands on the floor, palms down and about eighteen inches in front of your feet. Your fingers should be pointing straight ahead. Your arms should be coming down alongside your knees.

Begin the roll by straightening your legs and pushing forward with your feet. Let your weight ride forward easily. Immediately, put your chin against your chest. This will lower your head so that you can roll smoothly over onto your shoulders and down onto your back (Picture B). Your hands should still be on the floor.

But, as the roll carries you from your shoulders to your back (Picture C), bring your hands from the mat and grasp your shins. Pull your knees tight against you in what is known as the *tuck* position. The tuck will help you to keep turning smoothly until your feet reach the mat again.

Further, it will help thrust you upward to the standing position (Picture D) that ends everything. Because of the importance of the tuck to the whole exercise, the somersault is often called the *front tuck roll*.

The purpose of the exercise is to give you the experience of rolling

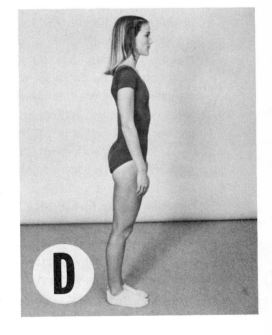

The Forward Roll

your body through a full circle. The roll should be done with no stops
or hesitations. And, to sharpen your balance, you should concentrate
on not leaning to one side or the other as you move.

Once you've practiced for a time, try a series of rolls, going nonstop from one to the other. Then it's time to start from a standing position. All in one flowing movement, drop to a squat and enter the
roll.

Exercise 2: The Backward Roll

Now, to give still more experience in rolling through a full circle,
let's travel to the rear. Start by squatting as before. But this time lean
forward a little and then push yourself back with your hands, sit
down, put your chin against your chest, and roll over on your back.

As soon as you're rolling along your back, move your hands to a
point just above your shoulders. Place them palms down on the floor,
with your fingers pointing toward your back. At the same time, to
help your momentum, bend your legs into a deep tuck.

When the roll reaches your shoulders and head, push your hands
hard against the floor. They'll propel you over and into a squatting
position. From there, end things by rising to your feet.

Don't worry if, at first, you find yourself stopping when the roll
reaches your shoulders. This is a common problem caused by lack of
momentum. You can solve it by rolling a little faster and by pushing a
bit harder with your hands. And remember, a very tight tuck position
will always help matters. Incidentally, the exercise is also known as
the *back tuck roll*.

As you did with your first exercise, try the backward roll in a
series after some practice. Then from a standing position.

Exercise 3: The Straight-leg Forward Roll

It's time to add to your agility by holding the legs straight as you
travel through a roll. No tuck at all this time.

The straight-leg forward roll can start from a squatting or a standing position. Let's experiment with the standing position. Set yourself
with your feet together and your arms above your head. Then forward you go. The pictures tell the rest.

The Straight-leg Forward Roll

Once you can roll forward with straight legs, you're ready to change direction and travel backward. Start from a squat, as you did in Exercise 2. Then it's up on your feet for a standing start.

Exercise 4: The Forward Straddle Roll

This exercise is a variation on the straight-leg forward roll. The variation is seen in the placement of the legs. Rather than being placed between your arms, they're going to be straddling them—that is, passing to their outside.

Start by standing with your feet about thirty inches apart and your arms outstretched. Bend forward, press your chin against your chest, and put your hands on the floor between your feet. Now, bending your arms, roll forward onto your shoulders.

Let the roll continue down your back. All the while, keep your legs stretched as wide apart as you can. Shoot your arms out straight to the front when the roll reaches your hips and brings you to a sitting position. Then drop your hands to the floor between your legs.

Finally, push your hands hard against the floor and lift yourself to a standing position. Your legs should remain stretched wide during the rise, and your feet should be thirty inches apart when you're again standing.

Exercise 5: The Backward Straddle Roll

Basically, this exercise is a forward straddle roll in reverse. Again (Picture A), you're in a standing position at the start, with your feet about thirty inches apart and your arms comfortably outstretched. Bend forward (Picture B), bring your hands between your legs, and place the hands flat on the floor.

Next, while supporting yourself on the hands, lower your seat to the floor. Once you're sitting, roll onto your back without stopping or hesitating.

Go right on rolling (Picture C) until you reach your feet (Picture D) and can rise again to a standing position. Keep your legs straight all the while. Bring your hands up alongside your shoulders for the final push that will complete the roll.

And need it be said? Try each straddle roll—the forward and backward—in a series as soon as you've practiced a bit. They're great fun.

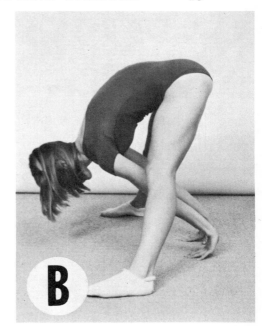

The Backward Straddle Roll

The Headstand

Exercise 6: The Headstand

Now let's put your balance to the test with a stunt that you probably tried for the first time when you were about two years old—the
headstand. Practically every infant has a go at it and ends up happily
falling into an accidental somersault. Here's how you could have
avoided that somersault.

You may enter the headstand from a squatting or a standing position. If you choose the former (it's a much easier start), first place
your hands on the floor about twelve inches in front of your feet. The
hands should be shoulders distance apart. The fingers should point
slightly outward.

Next (Picture A), drop forward onto your knees. Lower your head
until it touches the floor about twelve inches out in front of your
hands. Your hands will now be about level with your shoulders. Were
you to draw a line from both hands to your head, you'd find that it
would form a triangle. Be sure to maintain this triangle throughout
the coming movement. It will give you a solid base for keeping your
balance.

Raise your hips (Picture B) and carry them upward until your
back is straight. They'll bring your feet clear of the floor. For both balance and an attractive appearance, hold your legs in a tight tuck
against your chest.

Once your hips are directly overhead (Picture C), draw your legs
away from your chest. Keeping the knees bent, continue the movement until your upper legs are parallel to the floor. Then finish things
off (Picture D) by straightening the legs until your whole body is balanced vertically. To return to your starting position, simply reverse
the procedure.

It's all-important to keep your weight equally distributed on your
hands and head throughout the exercise. Too much weight on your
hands will prevent you from easily rising into the vertical position;
too much weight on the head will cause you to lose your balance. And
be alert to where the weight on your head is placed. If it's right at the
top or toward the back, you'll overbalance. The best spot is to the
front, a little above the forehead.

Once you've gathered some confidence, the entry from a standing position shouldn't prove too difficult. With one foot ahead of the other, lean far forward and place your hands and head in the triangular arrangement. Then kick the rear leg up to the vertical position, following it instantly with the leading leg.

Exercise 7: The Handstand

The kicking action that just carried you to a headstand can now help you perform what many coaches think to be one of the most difficult exercises in beginning gymnastics—the handstand.

Begin (Picture A) by positioning one leg ahead of the other and then bending forward until your hands reach the floor. Place the hands at shoulders width apart and about eighteen inches in front of your leading foot. Make a solid base for the coming move by spreading your fingers, pointing them ahead, and working your palms until they're firmly against the floor. Your arms should be perfectly straight.

Two cautions: First, be sure to lean your shoulders well forward at this time so that they're directly over your fingertips. A good lean is vital because it will help you to carry your legs and torso easily upward.

Second, pick a spot on the floor about twelve inches straight ahead and focus your gaze on it. Look right there as you kick upward. You'll keep your head from dropping and causing you to overbalance when you reach the top of the handstand.

Now for the kick itself (Picture B): Supporting yourself on straight arms, first send your back leg to the rear and up. Follow with your leading leg. The two should join as you near the vertical position. Carry them through the final inches until they're directly above your shoulders (Picture C). In their turn, the shoulders should still be leaning well forward. Your body should now be quite straight, with just a slight arch to your back.

Once in the handstand, you'll undoubtedly need to work your hands on the floor to secure your balance. But strive for the day when you can swing up into the handstand and hold it without any extra movement. In particular, try not to let your elbows or your knees

The Handstand

bend if you feel yourself sway or totter. These are bad habits that can cost you points in future competitions.

Since the handstand is one of the most difficult exercises in beginning gymnastics, you'll be wise to work with a spotter on your first attempts. The spotter can hold your legs in the vertical position while you grow accustomed to standing upside down. Or he can steady you whenever you begin to fall. You'll save all the time of having to start the exercise over and over again.

If you're alone, you can work alongside a wall. Swing upward until your feet are resting against the wall. Then, one at a time, slowly move them outward. Later bring them out together.

It's as tricky to come out of the handstand as it is to enter it. The return to your original position is accomplished by reversing the order of things. Bring one leg down at a time, landing on the ball of one foot and then the ball of the other. Gracefully straighten to a standing position. Don't let yourself drop both feet together. Not only will you look a bit clumsy but you'll also run the risk of stubbing your toes or losing your balance.

And what should you do if you lose your balance at any time? It all depends on where you are in the handstand. At times, it will be easier to give your body a half turn and drop to your feet. At others, you'll find it more comfortable to bend your elbows, tuck in your head, and drop into a forward roll.

Experience will show you how best to drop in a given instance of lost balance. At all times, though, remember to relax as you come down. Then you'll land gently and easily.

Exercise 8: The Cartwheel

Exercise 8 brings us back to the art of tumbling and one of the most classic movements in gymnastics. The cartwheel has been saved until now so that you could gain some experience in balancing on your hands before trying it.

You may perform the cartwheel to the right or to the left. The one explained here will send you to the left. You need only reverse the procedure if you wish to travel in the opposite direction.

When you're ready to try the exercise, take a moment to look along the floor and establish an imaginary line in your mind's eye. This is the path along which you'll travel. If you'll keep it firmly in mind, it will save you from veering off to either side.

Stand with your left side to the start of the line. Place your feet comfortably apart and stretch your arms up and out; for the best positioning, just imagine that your legs and arms are the spokes in a wheel. To gather momentum for the coming move, rock onto your right foot (Picture A) and then back to your left.

When you rock onto your left foot (Picture B), bend far over to the left from your waist. Place your left hand—palm down—on the imaginary line about two feet away from your left foot. At the same time, carry your right leg straight up and push off from the floor with your left foot.

As both legs swing overhead (Picture C), place your right hand on the floor a shoulder's width away from your left. You're now traveling through a handstand, with your arms very straight. If you have any trouble with balance at this point, try keeping your head arched well back. For a good arch, focus your gaze on a spot to your rear—midway between your hands but about twelve inches out beyond them.

Once you've passed through the handstand (Picture D), bend at the waist and aim your right foot downward to the imaginary line. Your left foot will automatically follow and land on the line. Your hands will leave the floor and you'll end (Picture E) standing with legs apart and arms outstretched.

You may have a little trouble keeping your legs straight on your first tries. And some trouble bringing them directly overhead. These are very common problems and can be corrected with a little practice. You'll find it much easier to keep the legs straight and bring them directly overhead if you'll hold them as far apart as possible.

And you may tend to veer off course. If so, you might try keeping your eyes on your hands throughout the cartwheel. This should help you stay on the imaginary line. It will also cut down on any tendency to let the body twist and pull you off course as your legs go up and over.

The Cartwheel

Exercise 9: The Front Scale

During floor exercises and on such pieces of equipment as the balance beam, you'll strike poses and balances that are very "dancelike" in appearance. Many of them are based on the balance known as the *scale*. So that you'll be ready to try them when the time comes, this chapter ends with the most basic of the scales—the *front scale*.

The front scale is a one-leg balance in which you lean your upper body forward until it is parallel with the floor. At the same time, the free leg is raised out behind you, and the foot—with the toes pointed gracefully—is carried to a point just above your head. Your head is held high, and your arms are extended forward or to the side.

Throughout the balance, your body is deeply arched. The arch runs all the way from the top of your head to the toes of your raised foot.

The front scale looks to be a simple balance. It is—but it is nevertheless an exacting and challenging one. You'll find that the job of standing on one foot with your body deeply arched will put your balance to quite a test. Likewise, your flexibility will be tested when you carry your leg so high that your foot is above your head.

When first practicing the scale, lift your foot just twelve inches or so up from the mat. Pause for a moment to check that you already have your body arched. Bring the foot up a few more inches, deepening the arch as you go. Pause for another check. Then continue until the foot is above your head.

*   *   *

All right. Now that you've practiced the nine beginning exercises, let's turn to your first competitive event—floor exercise. You'll have a chance to put the exercises to work and to add some new skills to your list.

The Front Scale

2 For Everyone— Floor Exercises

Floor exercise is one of the two events open to both men and women (the other, remember, is vaulting). The two sexes, however, do not compete against each other; men are always matched against men, and women against women. Yet they all do very much the same thing. Each presents a series of movements that gracefully demonstrates agility, flexibility, balance, and strength. The series of movements is called a *routine*.

THE EXERCISE AREA

Both men and women perform their routines in the same kind of area—a padded floor that measures a little more than thirty-nine square feet. In the United States, the floor is usually padded with mats one to two inches thick; a soft carpeting is placed over them to provide a single surface. For international competitions, special plates made of plywood are set down; they're covered first with a rubber material and then the carpeting.

No matter whether you're a man or a woman, your routine will be made up of movements of your own choosing. They should be carefully selected by you and your coach, with three points always being kept uppermost in mind:

1. Make sure that the movements blend together and flow easily from one to another. Then your routine will have a unified look to it that will impress the judges.

2. Make sure to choose a variety of movements. If you're to earn a

good score, your different skills must all be demonstrated. Some movements should emphasize agility. Some should emphasize flexibility. Some, balance. And some, strength.

3. Make sure that your routine carries you to every part of the performance area. Your score will be downgraded if you remain in just one or two spots the whole time.

Though the competitions for men and women are quite similar, they do have some differences. For instance, a man's routine must be performed in fifty to seventy seconds, but a woman is given from sixty to ninety seconds. Further, the woman puts much emphasis on graceful dance movements, while the man's attention is more on movements calling for strength.

Because of such differences as these, the chapter must now be divided into two sections—one for women, and one for men. But please, read both sections. Most of the movements explained in each can be performed by both men and women. To be a top gymnast, you should master as many as possible.

WOMEN'S FLOOR EXERCISE

Women gymnasts agree that floor exercise, which is always accompanied by music, is the most artistic of their four competitive events. It gives you the chance to become both acrobat and dancer. On the one hand, you perform all sorts of tumbling movements. On the other, you link them all together with a wide variety of dance movements.

Your music may be taped or live. If live, a piano is most always used. Live music is the wiser of the two choices because an accompanist can do something that is impossible for a taped selection to do— alter the timing to fit your needs. Perhaps, for some reason, you're performing a little more slowly than usual; or perhaps there's been a stumble or some other mishap. The taped music would go rushing right on, but not the accompanist.

Now let's see some of the tumbling and dancing movements that you'll be performing.

Tumbling Movements

The tumbling movements that you learned in chapter 1—from the forward roll to the head- and handstands—will all serve you well in floor exercise. To them you can add a variation of the forward roll. Best entered from a run, it's called the *dive forward roll to a stand.*

To enter the movement, run a few steps and then dive forward from both feet. As you fly through the air (Picture A), your body should be slightly bent, with your head and torso angling downward and your legs parallel to the floor. Land on both hands (Picture B), bend your elbows to cushion the impact, and tuck your head under. Immediately roll onto your shoulders (Picture C). Then keep right on rolling down your back (Picture D) until you come to your feet again (Picture E).

Many beginners have trouble with the diving part of the movement. It isn't that they think they're going to be injured; they're just not sure how far or how high they should catapult themselves. If you share this problem, there's a fun way to solve it. Have a friend get down on all fours. Then go sailing across her back.

Dance Movements

Dance movements are important because they serve as graceful bridges between your various tumbling stunts. They're so important, in fact, that your routine is allowed to run longer than a man's so that you'll have ample time to include them. In all, they round out your performance and give it a complete and polished look.

Before we talk further about dance movements, we need to do something else first. A few words must be said about posture and the way you walk.

Both are vital to good dance work—in fact, to good work *any-where* in gymnastics. Both help to keep you in balance. Both contribute to your co-ordination. Both give you a graceful and bouyant appearance.

Every good gymnast early develops the habit of holding the body erect when standing or walking. The head is always carried high. The shoulders are relaxed. The back is straight, the hips are tucked in, and

The Dive Forward Roll to a Stand

the buttocks are firmly set. The walk is firm but light, with the toes always gracefully pointed.

Keeping these points in mind, let's try some dance movements. The ones that are used in floor exercise can be divided into four categories. They are (1) dance steps themselves, (2) leaps and jumps, (3) poses and balances, and (4) turns.

Dance Movements: Steps

Many of the steps come from two fields of the dance—ballet and modern dance. Both are very broad fields, and so you can take your pick from many steps. And the ways in which you can blend and vary the steps often seem just about endless. As you become an expert gymnast, you'll be able to let your imagination and creativity take over in making your choices and deciding what to do with them.

To get you started, here is a trio of classic steps from the two fields.

Ballet Point (Pictures A and B): This simple but graceful ballet step begins (Picture A) as you stand with one foot slightly ahead of the other. Each foot is turned outward. Your weight rests on the rear leg, which is slightly bent at the knee.

Perform the step (Picture B) by simply sliding the front foot forward, pointing the toes, and bending your body over the foot. Your arms may be held as in the picture. If you wish, you may extend them to the sides or arch them overhead.

Ballet Touch (Picture C): This is no more than an extension of the ballet point. As you bend forward, let your arm swing gracefully downward until the hand touches your forward foot.

Body Wave (Picture D): The body wave is found in both ballet and modern dance. It is entered by bringing both feet together and going up on tiptoes. Incline your head forward, bend your knees, and swing your arms up to the front.

Now, as pictured, carry the arms downward and out behind you, at the same time pushing your knees and hips forward, and your head and shoulders backward. These actions give your body the wavelike motion that accounts for the name of the step.

The wave ends as your arms travel overhead. Straighten and rise up on tiptoes. From here, you can start the wave again with a bend of the knees.

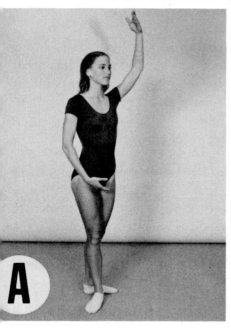

Dance Steps

Dance Movements: Leaps and Jumps

Just what is the difference between a leap and a jump? Basically, a leap carries you through the air for a distance, while a jump most often sends you straight up and down. The leap usually takes off on one foot and lands on the other. In the jump, takeoffs and landings may involve both feet or one or the other.

Shall we try some that all beginning gymnasts learn?

Cat Jump (Picture A): To prepare for this very simple jump, stand as you would at the start of the ballet point—with one foot in front of the other and each foot turned outward. Now up you jump, launching yourself from your left foot while bending your right knee out to the side. In the next instant, bend your left knee outward. While you're in the air, both feet will pass close to each other just below the torso.

Tuck Jump (Picture B): This time it's feet together at the start. Jump straight up, drop your head forward, bend your knees, and bring them as close to your face as possible. Swing your arms high to the rear. A good arm swing will help both the forward movement of your head and the upward thrust of your knees.

Running Leap (Picture C): Here is the most fundamental leap of all. It is entered from a short run of two or three steps, and the legs are fully extended to the front and rear as you sail through the air. Hold the back straight throughout the flight. Note that the arms are extended in the same manner as the legs.

With the flexibility that practice brings, you'll be able to move on to the *splits leap*. It's entered in the same way. But now, as you fly through the air, pull your legs up until they're in a splits position, parallel to the floor.

Stag Leap (Picture D): Now a real test for your agility and flexibility. After a run of two or three steps, take off from one foot and leap as high as you can. While in the air, extend the back leg out straight until it is almost parallel to the floor. At the same time, bend

Leaps and Jumps

the knee of your forward leg so that the foot rises to the upper area of the back leg. As on the other leaps, you may use any graceful arm position that you find comfortable.

Be sure to practice taking off from either foot so that you become adept at bending both the right and the left knee. And, of course, all the leaps should be practiced with the takeoffs from either foot.

Dance Movements: Poses and Balances

A pose is any statuelike position that is struck and held momentarily. Its chief purposes are three—to demonstrate grace, to "cap off" the preceding movement, and to give you an instant in which to prepare yourself for your next movement. A pose also demonstrates your flexibility.

A balance is, likewise, the holding of a position. But the position is held a little longer. And it is one that definitely challenges your sense of balance.

All sorts of poses are possible; in fact, there's nothing to stop you from making up some of your own. You'll be wise, though, to let your inventiveness wait until you're an experienced and skilled gymnast. First, put your mind to mastering the many poses and balances that all beginners must learn. Among them are the following:

Three Poses (Picture A): Here, in one picture, are three poses for you to try. It'll be a good idea to work in front of a mirror so that you can see exactly how you look and make any adjustments that may be necessary. Then you should begin to experiment with different ways to enter and leave the poses. For a start, why not try entering them from a forward roll and then the dive forward roll?

Scale Poses and Balances (Pictures B, C, and D): When you learned the front scale in chapter 1, you opened the way to a variety of poses and balances. Here are just three. Seen in Picture B is the *needle scale* balance. The *knee scale* pose is shown in Picture C, and the *abstract scale* balance in Picture D.

Poses and Balances

Turns

Dance Movements: Turns

Turns, of course, are movements that swing you in one direction or another. Some take you a quarter of the way around; some halfway around, so that you're facing in the opposite direction; and some in a full circle. Turns may be performed on the feet, the knees, the seat, or any other part of the body. Some may be done while you're in the air.

Standing Pivot (Picture A): Known as the *about face* to military men, this is one of the most basic of all turns. It is made on both feet and swings you around until you're looking in the opposite direction.

To begin, stand with one foot about six inches ahead of the other. Rise to the balls of both feet. Spin on them through a 180-degree turn by carrying your heels in a circling movement to the left. At the end of the turn, drop your heels back to the floor.

And that's all there is to it. But there are all sorts of variations waiting for some attention. First, try a series of pivots, dropping down from and then rising to the balls of the feet between each turn. Next, try walking into the pivot. Then walk into a series of pivots; take one step between each.

Finally, practice the pivot on one foot and then the other. Standing with your weight just slightly forward, rise to the ball of your front foot and bring the rear foot a few inches up from the floor. Then make the turn. With practice, you'll be able to swing not just halfway around but through a full circle.

Squat Pivot (Picture B): Here's still another variation. Simply squat down with one foot ahead of the other. Now onto the balls of the feet you go for the turn.

Whenever pivoting—whether standing or squatting—concentrate on keeping your back straight, your head high, and your hips firmly in place. Let your legs and feet do the work. Don't try to help matters along by sticking out your seat and whipping it around. You'll only present an unattractive appearance and—especially when squatting—run the risk of throwing yourself off balance.

Fouetté Battement (Pictures c and d): The fouetté battement is made on one foot and means a "kick with a turn." It can be performed on either foot, but we'll try it while balanced on the left.

Stand with the right foot to the front and your arms arched gracefully overhead. Kick the right leg smoothly forward (Picture c) until it is parallel to the floor. At the same time, rise to the ball of the left foot. Then pivot, turning the right foot downward as you do so. You'll end (Picture d) in the front scale, with your arms extended to the sides.

Sit Turn (Picture e): For our last turn, here's one that gives the feet a moment's rest. Sit with your legs so deeply bent to the front that your knees are level with your chest. Extend your arms straight ahead. Let your toes touch the floor.

Now, pulling your toes up from the floor, around you go in a full circle. Hold your arms, knees, and feet in place throughout the entire movement.

MEN'S FLOOR EXERCISE

As a man, you'll be expected to perform in pretty much the same manner as the women do. Though dance steps usually aren't as much of a feature in your routine, you'll still always be expected to move gracefully. And you'll be called on to perform movements that demonstrate flexibility, agility, and balance. In addition—as was pointed out a while back—you'll put a special emphasis on stunts requiring strength.

Let's start to build your routine with two movements that demonstrate flexibility.

For Flexibility

As seen in the pictures, the two movements may appear to be too simple for even the newest of gymnasts. But don't let appearances fool you. Both movements are going to do a real job of stretching

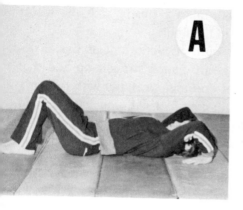
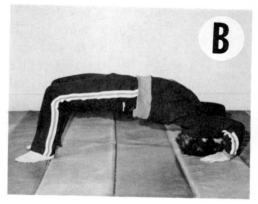

The Back Bridge and the Backbend

your back. You're going to need a very deep arch along the full
length of your spine.

Back Bridge (Pictures A and B): To prepare for the movement, lie
flat on your back (Picture A), with your knees together and bent.
Place your hands alongside your shoulders as you do in backward
rolls. Point the fingers at the shoulders and aim the elbows as straight
up into the air as possible. Press your hands and feet flat against the
floor.

Ready? Up you go by raising your hips and pushing hard against
the floor with your hands and feet (Picture B). Keeping the top of
your head against the floor, arch your back as deeply as you can. Hold

the position for a few beats. Maintain a very steady arch the whole time. Then slowly return your back to the floor.

The preparation for the bridge is quite as important as the movement itself. Be sure that your elbows are aimed straight up and that your hands and feet are perfectly flat on the floor. Only with properly aimed elbows and perfectly flat hands and feet will you have a solid base from which to thrust yourself upward.

A little at a time each day, practice pushing your midsection upward once you're in the bridge. You'll help matters along by pushing toward the center of the body with your hands and feet. Gradually you'll deepen the arch and give your back a flexibility that will serve you well in all areas of gymnastics.

The Backbend (Picture C): It's but one step from the bridge to the backbend, a stunt that further deepens the arch in your back. All you need do is straighten your arms and bring your head up from the floor. Your body should describe a high, continuous arch from your hands clear over to your feet.

Again, practice deepening the arch a little each day by pressing up on your midsection and pushing toward the center of the body with your hands and feet. But remember, just a little each day. Otherwise you're going to have some pretty sore muscles.

For Agility

A flexible back now joins with an agile movement of the feet and legs. The result is a basic floor exercise called the *squat through to a rear support.*

Start by dropping into the squat position. Lean your weight on your hands and immediately (Picture A) bring your feet up from the floor in a slight backward kick. Then let them ride forward between your supporting arms. Once the arms have been passed, straighten your legs. Stretch your body out and land (Picture B) in the rear support position. Your arms will be straight and supporting your weight; your back will be arched; and your head will be flung well back.

The job of carrying the body all the way through the movement nonstop never fails to cause problems at first. For instance, you can

The Squat Through to a Rear Support

be sure that the feet are going to bump into the floor somewhere along the line. And that the body isn't going to get itself fully straightened before you land in the rear support.

One way to overcome these problems is to practice the movement "a part at a time." First, after kicking your feet backward, let them swing forward and land right between your hands. Later, send them far forward so that you land in a sitting position. What you're doing here is building the agility necessary to carry you all the way through to the rear support.

As for the rear support, practice it all by itself until you've got it down pat and feel very comfortable in it. Then it's time to try the whole movement from beginning to end.

For Balance

Balances are very much the same for men as for women. We have seen the feminine versions of the needle and knee scales. Pictures A and B show what they look like in a man's routine.

Let's join them with two more balances that any gymnast—male or female—can perform.

Side Scale (Picture C): Here's another variation to add to your collection of scales. As in the front scale, one leg is extended to its full length, but the torso is turned to the side. One arm is held straight out alongside the head. The other runs down the body and along the extended leg. The side scale is often used as a balance just prior to entering a handstand, a headstand, or a cartwheel.

Swedish Fall (Picture D): In this movement, balance is combined with agility. From a standing position, drop straight forward, finally catching yourself on your hands and extending one leg high to the rear. On landing, bend your arms deeply and let your chest sink a bit toward the floor. Once you're completely in the balance, your body should be smoothly arched from your shoulders to your extended leg.

Balances

For Strength

Most strength movements end in balances. They're called strength movements because solid muscle power is required to perform the actions that lead up to the balances.

The four beginning strength movements that we'll now try all have one thing in common: Each begins from the squat position seen in Picture A.

Squat Headstand (Picture B): Drop down into the squat position, with the insides of your knees resting against your elbows, and your hands flat on the mat. Carrying your weight on your arms, you must now perform two actions simultaneously. First, lean forward until your head is resting against the mat. Second, raise your feet and bring them well clear of the floor.

Hold yourself in balance—on your head and hands, but with most of your weight on the hands—for several counts. Finish off by lowering your feet, raising your head, and rocking back to your starting position.

Squat Handstand (Picture C): Again, start in the squat position. Now forward you go. This time, however, don't lower your head all the way to the mat. Rather, lean forward until your chest is parallel to the floor. At the same time, raise your feet until you're completely balanced on your hands, with your arms supporting your weight. Hold the pose for a moment or two before slowly returning to your starting position.

The squat handstand may prove to be a bit difficult. Don't be disappointed if you keep toppling over on your first tries. Very soon, you'll learn the art of helping to maintain your balance by working your hands on the mat and pressing your fingers into it.

Press to a Headstand (Picture D): Let's go back to the squat headstand to talk about this one. Once you're in the squat headstand, it's quite easy to *press*—that is, raise your legs overhead—into a regular headstand. Simply bring the legs up as you did when practicing the

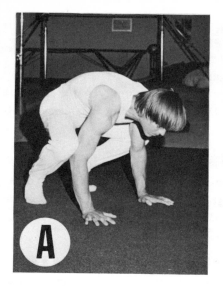

Strength Movements

headstand in chapter 1. As seen in the picture, first bring them up with the knees bent so that the upper legs are finally parallel to the floor. Then straighten the knees and send the legs up to a vertical position.

Press to a Handstand (Picture E): Now it's back to the squat handstand. You can press to a regular handstand from that position by first lifting the hips until they're above your shoulders. At the same time, bring the legs up with knees bent. Once you're in the position shown in the picture, extend the legs straight out vertically.

*   *   *

We've practiced twenty-seven floor exercise movements in this chapter. Practically every one of them can be performed by both men and women. All of them will give you the experience necessary to move on to more advanced work. Now it's time to get up on the balance beam.

3 A Women's Event— The Balance Beam

You run, dance, and pivot. You shoot forward into handstands. Sail through cartwheels and aerial walkovers. Your watchers can't help but gasp—because you're doing all these things on a narrow rail four feet above the floor.

That's excitement!

That's the balance beam!

THE BALANCE BEAM

The balance beam comes from Sweden and was first used back in the last century. Made of wood, it measures just over sixteen feet long. It is six inches deep and about four inches wide. Its surface is smooth—but never slippery—and its edges are rounded to avoid injury. In many competitions, the beam is covered with an elastic material to protect the gymnast even more.

Supporting the beam at either end are steel uprights. They hold the beam just about four feet above the floor. The best uprights are adjustable. Then the beam can be lowered for safety's sake during beginning exercises. Also, it can be dropped for younger children; they're allowed to compete on beams that are from two to four inches lower than normal.

GETTING STARTED

All sorts of movements can be performed on the beam. In fact, you'll be able to use practically every movement that you learn in tumbling and floor exercise. It's fun to transfer these various stunts to the beam. And greater fun to put the ones that you like best—or that challenge you the most—into a routine that will send you flowing back and forth along the full length of your "wooden tightrope."

The purpose of all beam work is to improve balance, grace, poise, and co-ordination. Balance, of course, is the very first thing that you'll be thinking about.

Correct posture is a must for balance. Just as you did when working on the floor exercises, remember to hold yourself very straight while walking or standing; as gymnasts say, keep the body fully extended. Carry the head high, with your shoulders relaxed. Keep your back straight, tuck in your hips, and set your buttocks firmly. As you stand, your weight should be right over your feet.

When walking, move confidently. Your legs should always be straight—except, of course, for those movements that demand a bend of the knees. Your feet should be slightly turned out to give you a secure grip on the beam. And your toes should always be pointed for a graceful appearance.

Let your arms move naturally as you walk. They'll automatically work to keep you in balance, swinging to just the correct heights or rising out to the sides. At all times, for an attractive appearance, hold your thumbs close in to the fingers.

Good posture and a correct walk will not only help your balance but will give you a graceful and buoyant look as well. You'll seem to be gliding or floating along the beam.

You'll probably want to climb up on the beam right away and get to work. But please remember that it's a wooden tightrope. You'll save yourself some unnecessary tumbles if you'll start your practice down on the floor. Spend some time walking a line that is about the width of the beam. At school, a sideline marker on the basketball court will do fine. At home, why not set down a line with masking tape in the garage? Then be sure to put in as much time walking backward as forward.

After some floor practice, you'll be ready to graduate to a low bench or—if your school has one—a low beam that is about twelve inches off the floor. Then, at last, you can try the high beam itself.

Once you're up there, keep walking backward and forward at different speeds until you're moving naturally and confidently.

As was suggested at the start of the book, you should use spotters whenever trying anything new on a piece of equipment. While you're getting acquainted with the beam, the spotter should move along the floor below with his or her hand extended up to you. He or she shouldn't take your hand but should only have hers or his there in case you need it. If your hand is taken, it is apt to pull you off balance.

BEGINNING MOUNTS

Once you've put in some walking practice, it's time to learn the correct ways to mount the beam so that you can begin your various movements. You may choose from any of several beginning mounts. The most basic one of all is the *front-support mount*.

Front-support Mount

To prepare yourself, stand facing the side of the beam (Picture A) and grip the top surface with both hands. Please study the grip closely. It's known as the *overgrip/across*.

Bend your knees and jump straight up so that you're supporting yourself on your arms (Picture B). Your arms and legs should be straight. Your body should be arched slightly, with your thighs pressed against the beam. Remember to point your toes and hold your head high.

Next (Picture C), swing one leg straight out to the side and bring it across the beam. At the same time, turn your body so that you end up (Picture D) straddling the beam as if it were a horse. Both legs should still be very straight and the toes pointed. Throughout the mount, your weight should be on your hands so that your body remains clear of the beam until you drop into the sitting position.

Your hands will shift as your body turns and comes down to straddle the beam. When the mount ends, they'll be holding the edges of the top surface (Picture D again) in the *overgrip/lengthwise*.

If you wish, you may use a springboard—it's called a *beatboard*—to help you with the mount or with the others that you'll be trying. Place the board alongside the beam. Then take a short run-in to the board and spring upward from both feet.

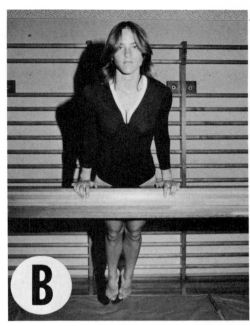

Balance Beam: Front-support Mount

Mounts from Feet-together Position

The front support mount is launched from a feet-together position. Several other mounts take off from this same position. Shall we give four of them a try?

Knee Mount (Picture A): Jump up, support yourself on straight arms, and bring one knee up until it is resting on the beam between your hands. As soon as the knee is in place, swing your other leg out to the rear and upward. Your foot, with toes pointed, should rise to a spot just above head level. The mount is completed when you make a quarter turn that faces you along the length of the beam.

Squat Mount (Picture B): Once again, jump up on very straight arms. But this time, lift your seat quite high, bend your knees deeply, and bring your feet onto the beam between your hands. Your shoulders should come in well over your upper legs. Hold your head high and straight to help your balance.

Wolf Mount (Picture C): Here's a variation of the squat mount—and one that's a bit more difficult to do. One leg comes up on the beam in the squat position between your hands. The other swings out to the side and is held horizontally above the length of the beam.

Straddle Mount (Picture D): This is a still more difficult mount that will give your balance a good test. All in one flowing movement, jump up, support yourself on straight arms, lift your seat high, and send your legs out to the sides so that your feet land outside your hands.

On your first tries, you'll have the feeling that you're overbalanced and are going to fall forward. It's a good idea not to attempt the jump until you have the "feel" of the straddle position itself. Climb up on a vaulting horse (see chapter 9) and get into the straddle position, holding it for as long as possible. Once you feel comfortable and balanced in it, then you can try your first jumps.

Mounts from Feet-together Position

A Running Mount

From mounts that can be launched from a standstill, let's turn to one that's done on the run. Gymnasts know it by either of two names: the *fence mount* or the *scissors mount*.

The mount calls for a beatboard to be placed alongside and almost parallel to the beam. Approaching on the oblique, run to the board and step up on it with your left foot. At the same time (Picture A), grip the beam with your right hand and swing your right leg straight up in front of you. Now spring from the board. Bring your left leg up next to your right and do a scissors kick. Supported by your right hand, let your body travel across the beam just as if you're vaulting a fence.

Everything comes to an end (Picture B) when you drop into the *side seat* or *stag position*. You're sitting on the beam with both legs over on its far side. The upper part of your left leg is on the beam itself, with the lower half dangling. The entire right leg is hanging straight down.

As soon as you can easily lead off with your right leg, you should reverse your approach and try the left. Accomplished gymnasts can lead off with equal ease with either leg.

The Fence Mount

MOVEMENTS, POSES, AND BALANCES

Once you've mounted the beam in competition, you'll rise and perform a routine made up of various movements, poses, and balances. The routine will run from 80 to 105 seconds. You'll be timed from the moment your feet leave the floor in the mount until the moment they touch it again on the dismount.

Your coach will help you develop a routine for competition. Great care should be taken in its planning, and you should keep three points uppermost in mind. First, plan to move continuously up and down the beam, with all actions flowing from one to the other. Second, plan to use the full length of the beam. And third, plan to put as much variety into the routine as your skill will permit.

To help you along your way to a fine routine, here are some of the movements, poses, and balances learned by all beginners.

Walking Movements

Plié (Picture A): The plié is a dipping step made as you're walking along the beam. Begin by walking naturally, pointing your toes and allowing your arms to swing freely. Then, on each step, dip slightly and drop one foot below the level of the beam. Though a very simple movement, the plié is a most graceful one when done correctly.

Side Step (Picture B): Here's a movement meant to give you the look of dancing. Just slide one foot along the beam and then slide the other foot until it catches up. The side step can be varied by crossing one foot in front of the other. Throughout, hold your hands and arms in a graceful and comfortable position of your choosing.

Goose Step (Picture C): This is one of the most classic steps in gymnastics. As you move along the beam, keep both legs stiff. The step can help to give your routine a light and humorous look.

In chapter 2, you learned such dance steps as the ballet point, ballet touch, and body wave. Now that you've practiced the side step, why not give them a try? See how gracefully you can move in and out of them as you travel along the beam.

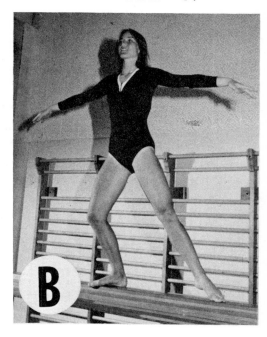

Walking Movements

Turning Movements

And you needn't stop there. The turns that you learned in chapter 2—the pivots and fouetté battement—can be transferred to the beam. Once you've tried them, you can go on to yet another turn. Like the fouetté battement, it's a kick turn.

The movement begins (Picture A) when you step forward onto your right foot as you're moving along the beam. Your arms are arched gracefully overhead. The left leg now executes two swings—first going to the front (Picture B) until it is parallel to the beam, and then riding back to the rear (Picture C).

As the left leg rises to the rear (Picture D), pivot to your left. Continue the pivot until you're completely turned in the opposite direction. Once the turn is completed, you may strike a pose or step along to another movement.

Kick Turn

Poses and Balances

Is there any need to say that the poses and balances in chapter 2 will all do fine on the beam? Here—starting with the *knee scale*—are three more poses.

And four new balances:

Poses

V-seat (Picture A): Requiring good muscular control in the legs and abdomen, this balance begins while you're sitting in a straddle position with your hands gripping the beam behind your back. It's done in two movements. First, bend your legs, bring your knees up to your chest, and carry your back and head forward to meet them. Second, straighten your back and head, and extend your legs straight out and upward. Hold the V-seat for several beats and then let your legs slowly return to the beam.

As you gain experience, begin to practice removing your hands from the beam once you're in the V. Soon, you'll be able to extend your arms out to the side while holding the position.

Forward Lunge (Picture B): As you face along the length of the beam, send one leg forward and bend it deeply at the knee. The rear leg is extended out to its full length. You may hold your arms in any graceful and striking manner.

Sideward Lunge (Picture C): Again, one leg is deeply bent and the other is held straight out. But this time the position is taken while your upper body is turned toward the side of the beam. Though the arms may be held in any graceful manner, most gymnasts prefer to extend them out to the sides.

One-leg Squat (Picture D): Drop down into a squat position, with one leg comfortably ahead of the other. Then, balancing yourself on the ball of the rear foot, lift the forward leg up from the beam, straightening it as you go. Hold the leg parallel to the beam for several counts.

Time for something different: Until now, you've transferred floor movements to the beam. But there's nothing to stop you from reversing the process. Why not take these new poses and balances down to a mat and try them there? They'll be nice additions to your floor-exercise skills.

Balances

Tumbling Movements

As it does on the floor, tumbling on the beam begins with the forward and backward rolls. Here's what they look like up on your wooden tightrope.

Forward Roll (Pictures A, B, and C): To begin (Picture A), drop into a deep lunge position, with your hands gripping the beam edges and your left leg extended high to the rear. Next, tucking your head in and bending your body sharply at the waist, roll onto your shoulders and then (Picture B) down your back. All the while, hold your legs very straight.

As you roll onto your shoulders, you'll need to shift your hands so that they can grip the underside of the beam. The new grip will help to propel you forward and along a straight line. At the end of the roll (Picture C), enter the V-seat position, with your arms extended forward and upward.

Once in the V, bend one leg, put your foot solidly on the beam, and rise to a standing position. If you wish, you may roll into the one-leg squat instead of the V-seat.

The Backward Roll (Pictures D, E, and F): Down onto your back you go (Picture D), with your body deeply bent at the waist and your legs extending straight past your face. Before beginning the roll, reach back and grip the underside of the beam.

Now, pulling against the underside of the beam, roll onto your shoulders (Picture E). At this point, your back should be vertical to the beam; your body should be bent at the waist; and your upper legs should be coming down past your face. You'll need now to shift your hands to the top of the beam so that you can more easily balance yourself as you complete the roll.

Let your feet come down until they touch the beam. End the movement (Picture F) by rolling until you're on your knees. Rise to a pose or to your next movement.

Forward and Backward Rolls

LEAPS AND JUMPS

In the eyes of many gymnasts, leaps and jumps are the most challenging of all the beam movements you'll learn as a beginner. You'll need to develop plenty of co-ordination, concentration, and accuracy for safe landings. But—as is true of anything challenging—there's great fun and satisfaction to be had in learning how to leave the beam so that one day you'll be able to sail through stag leaps and aerial walkovers.

All jumps and leaps, of course, should be practiced on the floor—and for a longer time than the other beginning moves. Working on a basketball sideline or a taped line, try the three beginning jumps that are described below. They'll contribute much to your balance and co-ordination. After some practice, you can transfer them to the beam and then begin to experiment with the leaps and jumps that you learned in chapter 2.

Straight Jump: Let's start with the most basic of jumps, though it is one that is quite graceful. Stand with your feet together. Simply bend your knees and jump straight up, pushing off from both feet at the same time. Your legs should be straight and your arms extended to the sides at the top of the jump. Come back down on the very spot where you were standing.

When first practicing, stick to small jumps only. Put all your concentration on going straight up and down and on landing steadily. Let height come with experience.

Change Jump: This is the ballet jump *changement de pieds* (meaning "changing of the feet"). Stand facing the length of the line, with the right foot in front of the left and with each pointed outward. Dip your knees and then push up from both feet. When you're in the air, open your legs slightly and cross them. You should land with your left foot in front of your right. Dip slightly on the landing.

Squat Jump: Squat down with one foot in front of the other. Now swing your arms up over your head and jump as high as you can. Your legs will automatically straighten. Bring them back to the squat position while you're in the air. You'll land on the beam in your original position.

DISMOUNTS

Every competitive routine ends with a graceful dismount that sends you from the beam to the mat. The dismount is highly important because it's the last thing that the judges see of your performance, and it should leave them with a very good impression. Also, it should be executed with such grace and flair that it becomes a high point of the routine—a high point that "caps everything off."

Your first practices should be spent simply dropping feet first from the beam as if it were a backyard fence. The whole idea is to get the "feel" of landing. You should jump with your arms positioned comfortably and then land on the balls of your feet.

On touching the mat, bend your knees to absorb the impact. Push down on your heels right away so that you end standing steadily on flat feet. Competition rules say that you must then straighten your legs, drop your arms to your sides, and come to attention. The judges will score you well if you do all this smoothly and with no excess movement.

Here now are two beginning dismounts—the *arch dismount* and the *cross-support dismount*.

Arch Dismount (Picture A): You can try this one from any point along the beam. It begins as you stand facing sideways, with legs straight and arms stretched to your front. Dip your knees and swing your arms downward and back to propel yourself into the air. Your arms swing back up high as you push off from the balls of your feet. In midair, arch your back deeply—right at the top of the jump. Land with arms outstretched and knees dipped.

Cross-support Dismount (Pictures B, C, and D): Here you should work at about center beam so that you don't hit one of the uprights as you're landing. Start by dropping into a knee scale. Grip the beam firmly. Then, to gather momentum for the dismount (Picture B), swing the free leg down and whip it back again.

As the free leg swings back, continue holding the beam, but straighten your arms. Likewise, straighten your kneeling leg. Pull it clear of the beam and shoot it up so that it is alongside the free leg. Your whole body (Picture C) will now be angled upward from the beam.

Let your body now swing downward alongside the beam. Land on dipped knees (Picture D), with one hand on the beam and the other upraised. Then come to attention.

Two Beginning Dismounts

4 A Women's Event—
The Uneven Parallel Bars

If you think the balance beam is exciting, wait till you try the uneven parallel bars. Now, instead of one wooden tightrope, you'll have two. And now, instead of walking and balancing and dancing, you'll go whirling around them and flying from one to the other.

THE UNEVEN PARALLEL BARS

The equipment consists of two round, wooden bars running parallel to each other above the floor. Each bar is usually about eight feet long. At their ends, both are attached to uprights that stand on metal or wooden bases. So that the uprights won't sway as you perform, steel cables are stretched tight from them and anchored into the bases or the floor.

The bars are called "uneven," of course, because one is higher than the other. The height of the high bar is just over 7½ feet, while the height of the low bar is just an inch under 5 feet. In top competitions, you may not alter these heights. You may, however, adjust them by a notch or two for lower-level meets so that gymnasts of all sizes are able to compete comfortably.

Though you may not tamper with the heights in top competitions, you're always free to adjust the distance between the bars. But only the low bar may be moved. You may shift it up to thirty inches away from its high companion. It must not be brought any closer than just over twenty-one inches.

The adjustment in distance is permitted for safety's sake. It enables gymnasts of different sizes to swing down from the high bar and always contact the low bar in the area where the hips bend. Without this safeguard, a woman could easily injure herself by striking the low bar either too far above or too far below the hips.

The uneven parallel bars are a recent addition to competitive gymnastics. At one time, women performed on the regular parallel bars, as the men still do. But work on the regular bars demands a great deal of strength—more than most women can comfortably produce. The women realized that, by raising one bar a couple of feet above the other, they could put the accent on flowing movements that called for grace, speed, and suppleness rather than strength.

The new bars appeared on the competitive scene for the first time in the late 1930s. They joined the Olympics in 1952. Today they are used by women gymnasts the world over and—thanks to the televised triumphs of Olga Korbut and Nadia Comaneci—are probably the best known of all gymnastics equipment to the general public.

GETTING STARTED

At the beginning of the book, it was suggested that, for as long as you're in gymnastics, you follow a regular program of exercises to develop agility, flexibility, stamina, and strength. A special word has to be said here about strength exercises.

Even though the uneven bars require less strength than the regular parallel bars, you're still going to need plenty of muscle power. The fact is that bar work demands more strength than any other of the women's events. And so, as you ready yourself for the bars, take time for some strength-building exercises.

Strength is going to be especially needed in the upper arms, the shoulders, the back, and the abdomen. Exercises that can be helpful include situps on the floor and liftups to a high bar. And be sure to talk with your coach. He or she will be able to suggest exercises that will best suit your needs and your body development at this time.

Your first sessions on the bars should be devoted to learning the simple movements that every newcomer must learn. They should be practiced individually at first. A little later, as you grow more skillful, you can begin to join some together. This will give you your first "feel" of what it will be like to perform a competitive routine.

A competitive routine is made up of from twelve to fourteen movements that send you circling and swinging around each bar, and traveling from bar to bar. The movements should be continuous, all flowing from one to another. There should be as few pauses as possible. If a movement does involve a pause, then the stop should be as brief as you can make it—no more, really, than a hesitation. Long pauses are sure to damage your score.

Even though all the movements demand strength, your routine at no time should ever make a show of that strength. Rather, the strength should always be hidden in the flow of the movements. What the judges should see is what they see in all skillful gymnastics events —a graceful, smooth, flowing, and continuous performance.

Basically, there are five kinds of movements in a bars routine. They are: (1) mounts, (2) circling movements, (3) swinging movements, (4) kipping movements, and (5) dismounts. Here we go with a beginning look at each.

BEGINNING MOUNTS

The first of the beginning bar mounts is quite similar—in fact, almost identical—to the first one that you tried on the balance beam. It's even called by the same name: the *front-support mount*.

Front-support Mount

Stand facing the low bar (Picture A) with your legs and back straight and your feet together. Extend your arms to the front and grasp the bar in what is know as the *regular grip* or, as it's also called, the *overgrip*. The fingers should be curled over the top of the bar.

To mount the bar (Picture B), thrust yourself upward with a bend of the knees and jump straight into the air. At the same time, push down on your hands. Straighten your elbows so that you end (Picture C) supporting yourself on straight arms. Your legs, likewise, should be straight and fully extended; please note how the toes are sharply and gracefully pointed. Let your weight rest on your upper thighs, causing your body to angle slightly across the bar. Hold your head and chest high, and your shoulders relaxed and down. From this position you'll be able to swing easily into any of several opening movements.

Uneven Parallel Bars:
The Front-support Mount

Three Mounts

Though the front-support mount will do for a start, it really isn't a very challenging one. The same can't be said for three other beginning mounts. Two of them will send you circling around the low bar. The third will start from the high bar.

Back Pullover Mount (Pictures A and B): Once again, standing with legs and back straight, face the low bar and grasp it in the regular grip. Launch the mount (Picture A) by pulling yourself forward with your arms and kicking one leg high beneath the bar. Immediately follow with the other leg.

With the legs together, carry them straight up (Picture B) on the far side of the bar. At the same time, pull your body up until you're touching the bar at the bend in the hips. Keep on pulling so that your legs and torso pass over the top of the bar. As your feet drop toward the floor again, call a halt to things with the straight-arm-support position.

Single-leg Swing-up Mount (Pictures C and D): You're going to circle halfway around the bar this time and end in a different support position. Everything starts as, facing and holding the low bar, you jump up and bring the left leg to a tuck position between your arms. Let your body swing beneath the bar (Picture C) while the tucked leg goes over the top of the bar.

At this point, your right leg—which is extended upward on the far side of the bar—comes into play. Whip it straight down and, in the very same instant, pull yourself up with your arms. These actions will send your torso arcing upward until you're on top of the bar. The mount ends there—in the *stride-support position*. As you sit straddling the bar and supporting yourself on straight arms, hold your left leg extended to the front, and your right to the rear.

Now, how about trying some variations? You can easily start by tucking the right leg over the bar in place of the left. Next, just back away a few steps and enter the mount from a run. Finally, don't tuck in the leg that you send over the bar; once the leg has passed between your arms, keep it straight.

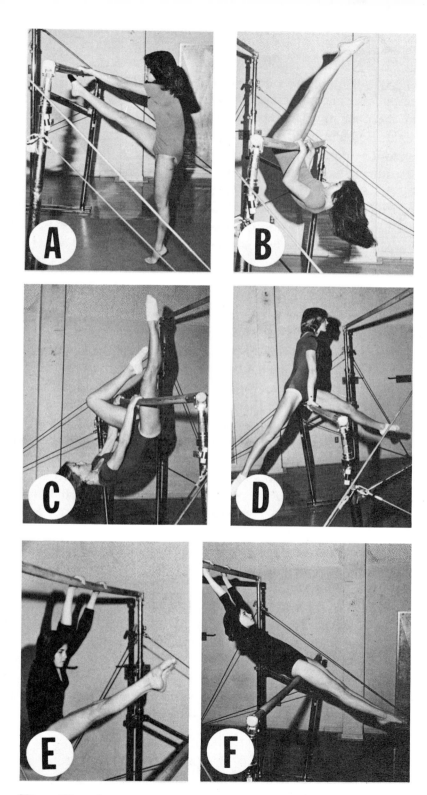

Three Mounts

Special attention must be paid to the hips when learning both the back-pullover and swing-up mounts. On the back pullover, be sure to send the opening kick high, right from the hip and with the leg straight. If you're to circle the bar easily, you must hold your hips as close to it as possible throughout the movement. A properly executed kick will help to get them up to where they belong.

Likewise, on the single-leg swing-up, whip the right leg downward right from the hip. And keep the leg straight throughout the whip. Good hip action and a straight leg—combined with a strong pull by the arms—will provide the momentum necessary to send you to the top of the bar.

Now let's try a mount from the high bar.

Hang from High Bar to Shoot over Low Bar (Pictures E and F): It takes almost as long to say its name as it does to perform this mount. Begin by standing beneath the high bar and facing the low bar. Jump straight up and catch the high bar in the regular grip.

To build the momentum needed for what comes next, swing your legs forward and then backward, keeping them straight the whole time. At the end of the backswing (Picture E), bring the legs up into a deep pike position by bending yourself sharply at the hips. Swing forward and let the legs pass above the low bar. Then straighten them so that the backs of your thighs (Picture F) drop against the low bar.

Still grasping the high bar, you'll end stretched across the low bar in the *rear lying position*. Your legs should now be fully extended and your toes sharply pointed.

Two variations: First, enter the mount from a run of several steps. Second, instead of keeping your feet together, sail across the low bar in the straddle position.

Good abdominal strength is needed to pike the legs for the shoot over. You'll be wise to build that strength gradually by hanging from the high bar and first pulling the legs up to a tuck position. As strength builds, extend the legs out from the tuck to the pike position. Then, when the time seems right, skip the tuck and go directly to the pike. If you still don't have the necessary strength when you try the mount itself, you can go on using the tuck for a while longer.

CIRCLING MOVEMENTS

Just as their name indicates, these are movements that send you around the bar. They are performed as though your arms, legs, and torso are the spokes in a wheel, with the bar serving as the hub. Whenever doing them, always remember to help yourself along by rotating your hands on the bar.

In this section, we'll work on three circles. Two are launched from the front-support position. The third starts from the stride position. After you've practiced them individually, you can begin to combine them with the appropriate mounts.

From the Front-support Position

Hip Circle Forward (Pictures A, B, and C): The first move here will put your balance to a nice test. Let yourself ride forward (Picture A) from the front-support position until you're stretched right across the low bar, with your torso and legs parallel to the floor. Now (Picture B), bending sharply at the hips, drop your head and torso toward the floor. Swing below the bar. Then, with your hips following, circle the bar (Picture C) until you return to the front-support position.

Throughout the movement, your hip joints should be right at the bar. Rotate your hands as you go. Bring your wrists over the top of the bar as you come up and prepare to enter the front support.

After you've practiced for quite a time, you'll be ready to try two very exciting variations. Start the first by releasing your grip and extending your arms straight past your head as you stretch out horizontally on the bar. Then enter the circle by swinging the arms down forcefully and piking the body. Regrasp the bar as you pass through the circle. End, as usual, in the front-support position. The movement is called the *free forward hip circle*.

In the second variation, the arms are again extended and whipped downward to send you into the circle. But now they do not regrasp the bar. Instead, as you travel around, they rise to catch the high bar. You leave the low bar and end hanging from the high bar.

Hip Circle Backward (Pictures D and E): To launch this movement, break out of the front-support position by swinging your legs back and forth to gain momentum. Then (Picture D) lift them high to the rear. Straighten your arms and push yourself up from the bar as you do so.

Keep the legs straight and together as they arc down from the backswing. On reaching the bar (Picture E), let them curl beneath it. Pike your body and send the legs rising up the far side. Continue the circle, moving your hands as you travel, until you return to the front-support position.

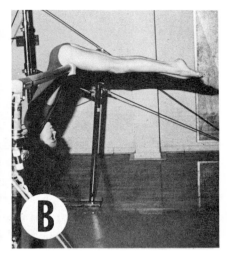

Hip Circles

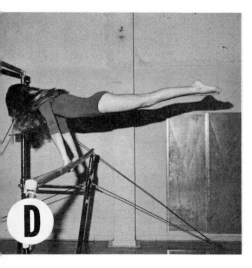

From the Stride Position

The movement that we'll try here is the *mill circle forward*. Before performing it, you'll need to change your hold on the bar. As soon as you're in the stride-support position, turn your hands into the *reverse grip*. Place your thumbs to the front—in the direction you'll travel— and curl the fingers around the back of the bar.

Prepare for the circle (Picture A) by pushing down on your hands and lifting yourself slightly from the bar. Arch your back and bring your chest well forward so that it's ready to lead the way through the movement. Hold your head high. Your legs should be in a wide-split position.

Leading with your chest (Picture B), swing your torso forward and downward. As you drop, let the bar rest against the thigh of your rear leg. Shift your hands to help you on your way and (Picture C) pass beneath the bar. Continue circling up the opposite side (Picture D) until you're back in the original stride-support position.

It's all-important to keep the back arched so that the chest is well forward throughout the circle. Unless the chest is leading, you'll hinder the momentum needed to see you all the way around the bar. Straight legs and a head held high also contribute to maintaining your momentum—and, of course, to presenting a graceful appearance.

A variation for a future day: As you become a more experienced gymnast, you'll be able to incorporate the high bar in the circle. Travel around the low bar for three quarters of the way. Then quickly reach up and grab the high bar with both hands. You may then transfer to the high bar or enter some appropriate movement.

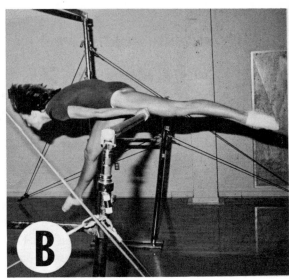

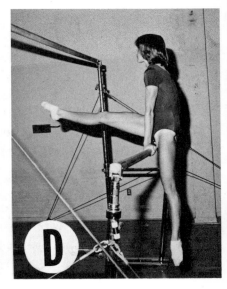

The Mill Circle Forward

SWINGING MOVEMENTS

Swinging movements are performed as you hang from a bar as if it is a tree limb. With them, you may travel all or part of the way around a bar, or from bar to bar. Very often, swings are combined with circles to produce some of the most exciting stunts in gymnastics.

The Cast

The cast is the most basic of the swinging movements, one that every gymnast must learn. It's the method by which you launch and build a swing from a standstill. The fact is that—without knowing it—you performed a cast a moment ago in the hip circle backward. It came when you swung your legs back and forth and then pushed yourself up from the bar at the start of the swing.

Let's repeat what you did, this time taking your actions a step at a time.

The cast may be performed on either the low bar or the high bar. On the low bar, it is launched from the front-support position. Bending slightly at the hips, send the legs back and forth beneath the bar. Then, with the shoulders well forward over the bar, carry the legs high to the rear. Push yourself up from the front-support position so that you're an arm's length away from the bar at the height of the backswing. Keep the body extended as the legs drop back down to the bar.

When first practicing on the low bar, work with your back to the high bar. Start with low swings. Then slowly build the height of the swings until your legs are touching the high bar.

The cast also begins from the front-support position on the high bar. Swing your legs back and forth beneath the bar. Enter the backswing and push yourself up from the bar. But now—as you reach the top of the backswing—give your shoulders a slight thrust away from the bar. This action will cause your legs, torso, and arms to be fully extended and parallel to the floor. Then keep the body under firm

The Cast

control as, hanging full length, you swing down and beneath the bar. The full-length hang is called a *long hang*.

The cast is such a basic movement that, once it is learned, it should be practiced daily as part of your workout program or as long as you're a gymnast.

Now let's combine the cast with a circle. The result: the very exciting swinging movement called the *flying hip circle*.

Flying Hip Circle

The movement starts in the front-support position on the high bar. Cast and swing down (Picture A) through a long hang. When you strike the low bar at the hips (Picture B), shoot your legs forward in a pike and whip them up the far side of the bar. In the same instant, release the high bar and catch the low bar alongside your hips. Your momentum will carry you through a backward hip circle (Picture C) to a front-support position on the low bar (Picture D).

The flying hip circle qualifies as one of the more difficult beginning movements. For safety's sake, it should be practiced a step at a time until you're comfortable in each step. First, hang from the high bar and swing back and forth, touching the low bar and swinging your legs into the pike position. Don't release the high bar at this time, but simply grow accustomed to piking in the instant that you strike the low bar.

After some practice, you can begin releasing the high bar. Again, swing back and forth while in the long hang. On every third or fourth contact, release the high bar and perform the hip circle.

Finally, practice dropping from the cast, striking the low bar, and piking the legs. No release just yet. Continue practicing until you've got everything down pat. Then you can take the biggest step of all and put the whole movement together from beginning to end.

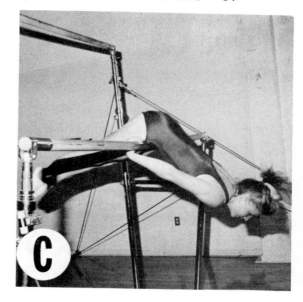

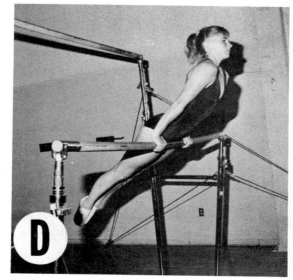

The Flying Hip Circle

KIPPING MOVEMENTS

In general, a kip is the movement that carries you from a hanging position to a position in which—as in the front support—you're up on your arms. It's helped along with a pike and usually sends you from one bar to the other. Kipping movements are among the most spectacular stunts in advanced gymnastics. To prepare for the day when you can perform them all, you'll need to start with the following two.

Double-leg Stemrise (Pictures A and B): This simple kip begins as you're grasping the high bar (Picture A) while resting the feet on the low bar. All you need do (Picture B) is push against the low bar with the balls of your feet and straighten your legs until your hips are up against the underside of the high bar. Then pull free of the low bar with a slight pike. End by moving into a front support on the high bar.

Single-leg Stemrise (Pictures C, D, E, and F): Though still quite easy to do, this kip is slightly more difficult than its double-leg relative. Start in the rear lying position with your hands grasping the high bar and your back across the low bar, as if you've just completed a shoot-over mount. Now (Picture C) bend the right knee and place the right foot on the low bar. This action automatically draws the left leg up until it is resting on the bar and is parallel to the floor.

Two actions are now performed in quick succession. First (Picture D), kick the left leg high. Second, as you're bringing the left leg back down, straighten the right leg (Picture E) and carry your hips up to the underside of the high bar. The actions end as you lift both feet away from the low bar, pike the body slightly, and end (Picture F) in the front-support position.

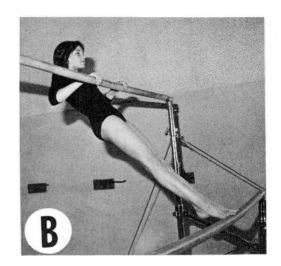

Kipping Movements

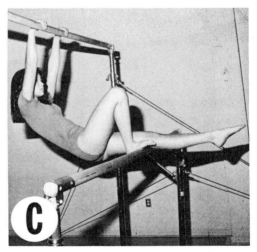

DISMOUNTS

The basic rules for dismounting the uneven parallel bars are the same as those for the balance beam. Swing gracefully through the dismount to land on the balls of the feet. Cushion the impact with a bend of the knees. Drop the heels to the floor immediately and come to attention.

There are more than twenty-one different ways to dismount the bars. They start with the two that we'll now learn.

Cast Off from Front Support (Pictures A and B): From the front-support position swing your legs beneath the low bar and then back into a cast (Picture A). At the top of the cast, push away from the bar, thrust yourself clear, and drop (Picture B) to a bent-knee landing.

Underswing from High Bar over Low Bar (Pictures C and D): For our final movement in the chapter, here's a dismount that incorporates both bars. Starting in a front support on the high bar, push yourself up and back by straightening the arms. At the same time (Picture C), pike the body deeply. As you now swing beneath the high bar (Picture D), extend the body and aim your legs up over the low bar. Release the high bar as your legs are rising so that you can arc over the low bar to a landing. Exciting, right?

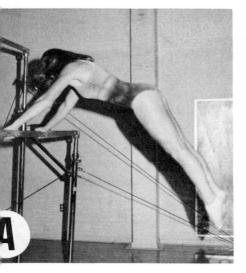
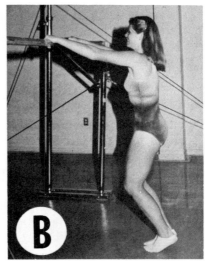

Two Dismounts

5 A Men's Event— The Rings

The rings are often called the brother of the flying trapeze. Besides looking somewhat alike, both pieces of equipment came into being in the early 1800s. Both were invented by the same man—Francis Amore of Spain.

Since then, the trapeze has become a mainstay of circus entertainment, providing thrills for audiences all across the world. The rings have found a place for themselves in gymnastics and, in their own way, have provided just as many thrills. Audiences are always left breathless by the spectacular upper-body strength that enables a ring man to hang motionless for long seconds above the gym floor after he has stretched his arms wide in the iron cross position.

Just how much upper-body strength will you develop if you enter this activity and then stick with it? More than you'll ever require for any other gymnastic event. Many ring gymnasts say that they need quite as much arm and chest strength as the Vassili Alexeevs of this world use in weightlifting.

THE RINGS

Gymnasts once competed on metal rings covered over with leather to protect the hands. Since the mid-1950s, though, rings made of smooth, laminated hardwood have been steadily replacing the old-fashioned metal ones. The wood measures 1⅛ inches in diameter. The inside diameter of each ring is 7 inches.

For competition, the rings hang from a beam that is set 18 feet above the floor. The rings themselves are 8 feet, 2½ inches above the floor—with this measurement being made from the bottom of each ring—and are a little more than 19 inches apart. Each ring is attached to a leather or nylon strap. The strap runs up to a steel cable that then goes the rest of the way to the beam.

A swivel device in the beam permits each ring to turn in continuous circles. The rings are also able to swing freely backward and forward.

Most gyms are equipped with competition and practice rings. The practice rings usually hang from 4 to 6 feet above the floor because it is easier and safer for the learner to work at these heights. Floor mats should always be in place during practice sessions, and a spotter should always be on hand.

GETTING STARTED

Many young people are surprised when they approach the rings for the first time. They expect to go swinging back and forth, just as if they were on a trapeze. The coach quickly tells them that nothing could be farther from the truth.

There was a time when you could swing through the air in what are called flying-ring events. But—in great part because of the dangers involved—they were dropped from most competitions back in the 1960s. Today's gymnast participates in *still-ring* events. He performs a routine made up of various exercises—presses, balances, and even swinging movements—while holding the rings in as stationary a position as possible.

All the exercises in a competitive routine can be divided into two basic types: *hold positions* and *swinging parts*. Just as their name indicates, hold positions are those that you get into and then hold for a time. Actually, each must be held for at least two seconds to win you a good score.

Swinging movements, of course, are actions that your legs and torso swing through, often to get you into positions that you will then hold. These actions must be accomplished without shaking or swinging the rings too much. And they must be performed smoothly, without extra or unnecessary body action. If done properly, they're grace-ful to see and will always earn you a high score.

The hold positions will develop great strength in your arms, shoul-ders, and chest. But suppleness will also be developed—thanks to the twisting and turning that must be done during many of the swinging actions. And you can count on building up tremendous strength in your hands; they're going to spend their time supporting your entire body weight.

Get-acquainted Exercises

Now let's try a few exercises meant to get you acquainted with the rings. Please don't head for a competition set and try to jump up and grab them; you won't get a good hand grip and you'll run the risk of painfully stretching some muscles. Rather, simply stand between practice rings that are hanging at about shoulder height. With your back straight and feet together, take the rings securely in the *regular grip* (Picture A). The hands hold the rings with your fingers toward you. Once you've tested the grip and set your hands comfortably, it's time to begin.

Standing Chin-up (Picture A): All that you need do here is use your shoulders to pull yourself straight up. At the top of the chin-up, your hands are alongside your jaws. Your arms are in a deep V. Your legs are together and straight, with your toes pointed right at the floor. Hold the position for a beat or two and then lower yourself slowly until you're standing again.

Throughout the exercise, you'll probably feel a heavy strain on your shoulders and arm muscles. The strain will lessen over the next days as you repeat the exercise and increase your strength. Do not try to hurry things by repeating the exercise too often on any one day; you'll only end up with stiff muscles. Rather, build your strength gradually by increasing the number of chin-ups a little each day.

Kneeling Chin-up (Picture B): Once your arms begin to gather strength, you can start the chin-up from an actual hanging position. To get into this position on the practice rings, simply bend your legs under you so that you're kneeling in the air. Then pull yourself straight up as before. Let your legs straighten at the top of the chin-up. Bend them again as you come down.

Half-lever Chin-up (Picture C): Here's an exercise that will test your strength a bit more and give you some beginning experience in making a swinging action. It's done in two steps. First, raise your legs until they're parallel to the floor in the half-lever position. Then pull yourself straight up into the chin-up. Hold your legs in the half-lever position until you've lowered yourself back to your starting position.

Throughout, concentrate on moving as smoothly as you can. Try not to disturb or shake the rings in any way.

The exercise should first be done from a standing position. Then, to start from a hanging position, bring your legs up against your chest in an upside-down V before straightening them to the half-lever position.

Arm-to-the-side Chin-up (Picture D): From a standing and then a hanging position, pull yourself into the chin-up. Then extend one arm

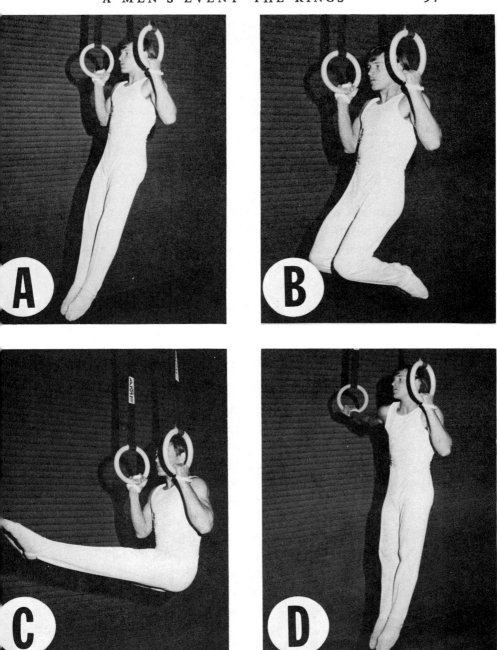

The Rings: Get-acquainted Exercises

straight out to the side. As the arm goes out, turn the ring so that the back of your hand is toward you. At the same time, flatten the hand as if you're a boxer about to jab an opponent.

Draw the arm back and then extend the opposite arm to the side. Again, concentrate on working very smoothly. Try not to shake the rings. Early practice in this direction will win you good scores later.

SWINGS AND HOLDS

Beginning swings and holds are all done from a hanging position. This position is used at the start because the act of hanging from your arms requires just ordinary strength and will not put a dangerous strain on you. More advanced work involves the support position, in which you go up on your arms, with your weight then pressing down on them. Though you can easily use the support position as a beginner in other events, it demands a far greater strength on the rings.

Here are some beginning swings and holds for you to try. They're all fun to do and can be blended into a routine when you enter your first competition.

Pendulum Swing

The pendulum is really much more than just a beginning swing. It's a basic action that you'll be using time and again in all your routines.

All routines begin with the gymnast in a motionless position. The pendulum gives you the momentum necessary to enter your first swings or to rise to many of your first holds. Later you'll need its momentum to carry you from the end of one movement into the beginning of another.

The actions of the pendulum must be performed with a great deal of control. They should cause the body to gather momentum, but they should disturb the rings only slightly. Remember, the rings must remain as motionless as possible at all times.

As you're hanging from the rings (Picture A), start by bending at the waist and raising the legs forward. Hold the legs straight as you bring them up, and then be sure to keep them straight throughout the rest of the swing.

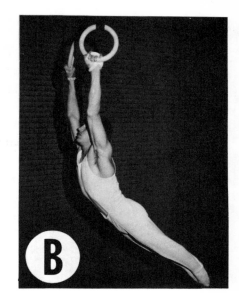

The Pendulum Swing

Once the legs are parallel to the floor, let them drop down and back (Picture B) until your body is arched. Then, really gathering momentum, bring them forward and up again. To "cap off" the momentum, bend slightly at the waist as you're rising, and pull up on your arms so that (Picture C) your body is raised toward the rings at the top of the forward swing. At this point you may enter a movement if your momentum is sufficient, or you may drop the legs and arc down (Picture D) into another backswing.

Your momentum can be increased on each swing by the pumping action of bending at the waist, pulling up on the arms, and raising the body. The increasing momentum, of course, will carry you higher and higher at the end of each swing.

Now let's use the pendulum to carry you up to your first hold.

Two Hold Positions

The first hold is called the *bent body inverted hang*. It's one that you'll use quite often. You can present it by itself as an individual hold in your routine. More often, you'll approach it or pass through it while performing other movements.

The hold is seen in Picture A. Using the pendulum swing, send your legs upward and between the straps holding the rings. Then straighten the legs so that they're parallel to the floor and right above your face in the hold itself. Your eyes should be looking directly up at your knees.

Remain in the hold position for several counts. Then, to return to your starting point, simply reverse the process. Keep the legs straight as you come down.

Now what about Picture B? Shown is a hold that's almost identical to one of the chin-up exercises—the *hanging half lever*. It's a nice one to enter as you're coming down out of the inverted hang. Simply stop your legs when they're parallel to the floor. Your back should be perfectly straight throughout the hang.

If you wish, you can vary things by performing the half lever first and then swinging up into the inverted hang.

Two Hold Positions

Two Swinging Movements

Here now are two swinging movements that you've probably done at one time or another on playground rings. Now you can use them as a gymnast.

Skin-the-cat (Picture A): Again, using the pendulum for momentum, swing your legs up until they pass between the ring straps. But this time, don't stop when your knees are above your eyes. Let your legs continue on their way until they're pointing back down toward the floor. A reverse of the process returns you to your starting position.

The Bird's Nest (Picture B): Up your legs go again, this time until they're just passing between the ring straps. At this point, turn your feet outward and catch the rings with your insteps. Then arch your body deeply, with your face looking right down at the mat.

How about trying a variation? Remove your left foot from its ring and extend the leg straight out to the rear.

Another Hold Position

Here's a beginning move that will give your muscles and sense of balance a real test. It's called the *straight-body inverted hang.* Many gymnasts also know it as the *inverted layout hang.*

Begin by bringing your legs up between the ring straps as if you're planning to enter a bent-body inverted hang. But, just as your knees are passing between the straps (Picture A), push your legs directly toward the ceiling. In the same instant, straighten your body so that you end (Picture B) hanging upside down, with your head aimed right at the floor.

At first you may experience some difficulty in holding your balance while upside down. It's all right to rest your feet against the ring straps to help keep your balance until you're accustomed to things.

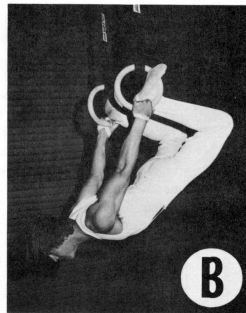

Skin-the-cat and the Bird's Nest

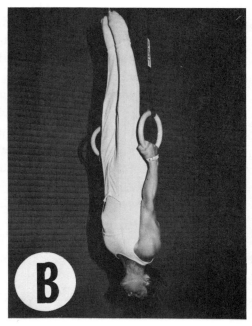

The Straight-body Inverted Hang

Another Swinging Movement

The single-leg cutoff is perhaps the most challenging of the beginning movements. It starts when you swing yourself up into the bent-body inverted hang.

Now, to give yourself the momentum needed for the coming action, lift your hips and point your legs down across your face and toward the floor. Next (Picture A), swing them back toward the ring straps. As you do so, keep your left leg in a line that will carry it between the straps. But extend your right leg out to the side (Picture B) so that it will pass on the *outside* of its strap.

Your right leg will strike your right arm—and here comes the tricky part.

As the leg touches the arm, let go of the ring and drop your right hand. The leg will then travel past the outside of the ring and through the open space left by your dropped hand. At the same time, the left leg will pass between the straps.

Once your right leg is through the opening, grasp the ring again. Bring your legs together and let your body continue downward until you're hanging vertically.

It's vital that your head be held correctly throughout the movement. It should be forward, with your chin almost on your chest. This position will help to carry you forward through the swing. And your eyes will always be on the ring so that you'll be able to catch it quickly once the leg is past.

After you've practiced for a time with the right leg, you can vary things by switching to your left. Then—for a truly striking variation —why not try the *double-leg cutoff?* Send both legs out to one side during the swing. Release the ring and let the *two* legs pass on the outside of the ring and through the opening.

The Single-leg Cutoff

MOUNTING AND DISMOUNTING

Unlike the balance beam for women, there are no fancy ways to leap up to the rings and begin your routine. If you wish, you may stand under the rings and simply jump up to a hanging position. Most gymnasts don't like to do this, however. The rings should be completely still at the start of the routine, and the jump does nothing but disturb them. Then you have to hang there until they're quiet again.

It's best to have your coach or a teammate stand behind you and then lift you to the rings. He'll hold you up until you signal that you've got a secure grip and are ready to work. When he releases you, he'll do so gently so as not to disturb the rings. As soon as he steps away, your routine officially begins.

There are, however, several very exciting ways to dismount the rings. Most of them require more skill and strength than you can be expected to have as a beginner, and so should be saved for a later date. Let your coach be your guide as to when you're ready to try them.

In the meantime, you can concentrate on a simple—but very attractive-looking—dismount. It's called the *backward-straddle dismount.*

Backward-straddle Dismount

What you're going to perform is a backward-straddle roll in the air; in the middle of it, you'll let go of the rings and drop feet first to the mat. To see how it works, let's say that you've just completed the single-leg cutoff. You've grasped the ring again, and your body is arcing downward toward a vertical hang.

As your legs come down, straighten them forcefully to give yourself some momentum. Then, as soon as the legs are hanging vertically, use that momentum to help pump them backward (Picture A). Follow that backward pump with one that brings you forward and carries your legs upward—piked and in an arc—to the ring straps.

As the legs are rising (Picture B), shoot them out to the straddle position so that they'll pass to the outside of the straps. Then, as

Backward-straddle Dismount

they're passing the straps, pull hard to lift your body. Throw back your head and release the rings (Picture c). Keep the legs traveling in an arc overhead. Then, completing the roll, let the legs drop floorward for the landing (Picture d).

Though the dismount is a beginning one, it will need plenty of practice before you've got it down pat. For safety's sake, learn it a step at a time. Start from a vertical hang and—after getting yourself moving with few pendulum swings—do nothing more than work on carrying your legs upward in the straddle position. Next, at the top of each swing, practice pulling hard on the rings and throwing your head back. Both actions are vital to the dismount. The first lifts you to a high point for the release. The second—and also the upward pull— helps to keep your legs traveling through the arc overhead.

Once you've accustomed yourself to all these "lead up" actions and can perform them smoothly, it will be time to try the dismount from one end to the other.

Dismount Landings

Before you attempt the dismount, your coach will undoubtedly talk to you about the correct way to land. All landings should be made on the balls of the feet, with the legs close together. Both feet should strike the mat at the same time. The knees should bend to absorb the impact, and the body weight should be slightly forward for balance. You may hold your arms in any manner—up, out to the sides, or forward—that is comfortable and that provides good balance. Later, the arm positions will often be determined by the type of dismount you use.

It's a good idea to practice your first landings by jumping from a low bench. Good competition form requires that you come to attention as soon as you land. So quickly develop the habit of straightening your legs immediately after impact. Then, all in one flowing movement, drop down from the balls of your feet, bring your hands to your sides, and snap to attention. Hold the pose for a moment before leaving the mat.

6 A Men's Event— The Side Horse

Back in the 1700s, European riders used a wooden horse for practicing the stunts they would later try on the real thing at a full gallop— stunts such as standing on your head in the saddle. The wooden horse was about five feet high and had legs, a head, and even a tail. Midway along its back, leather straps formed the outline of a saddle. In time, the head and tail were removed as unnecessary. The horse went on helping riders until well into the next century.

One rider to be helped in the 1800s was Friedrich Jahn, who practiced on the horse while in the German Army. Later, when he was teaching gymnastics, he decided that the horse could be used for some excellent exercise by his students. He streamlined the creature and replaced the saddle straps with two curved handles, called pommels. His invention was a success not only among his pupils but also among gymnasts everywhere. It is still with us today and is known in the United States as the *side horse*.

THE SIDE HORSE

We Americans are just about the only people in the world to call the horse by this name. In most other countries, it's always been the *pommel horse*. Our name comes from the fact that the exercises performed on the horse are all done from along its sides.

The horse stands on metal uprights that are attached to a heavy base so that it will not shake during the exercises. Its torso—or top section—is made of wood that is padded with felt and covered over with leather. The top section measures from 63 to 64 inches long. It is about 14 inches wide. American horses stand on two uprights; most foreign models have four.

The pommels are 4¾ inches high. Usually they are adjustable and can be set from about 16 inches to a little under 18 inches apart. The height of the horse—48 inches—is measured from the top of the pommels to the floor.

As you stand looking at the horse from the side, you'll see that the pommels divide the top into three areas. Each area is known by two different names. Straight ahead, between the pommels, is the *saddle* or *center section*. To your left (no matter which side you're standing on) is the *neck* or *left end,* while the *croup* or *right end* is over opposite. Though you may use whichever set of names you wish, many coaches and gymnasts look on *neck, saddle,* and *croup* as being pretty old-fashioned.

GETTING STARTED

If you'll stick to side-horse work once you've started, you'll be able to count on two benefits. First, you'll develop some fine muscles in your shoulders, arms, and wrists. But you probably won't build especially large muscles with the sort of bursting power that is needed for, say, the rings or weightlifting. Instead, the muscles will tend to be wiry. Second, you'll develop your sense of balance, your muscular control, and your stamina. By the time you become an experienced side-horse gymnast, they should be just about as sharp as can be.

Why can you count on all these benefits? Because you'll be performing competitive routines that will see you in constant motion. Nonstop, you'll work your way up and down the full length of the horse. All the while, you'll swing your legs through half circles, full circles, and various scissor kicks. Some circles will be made with just one leg at a time. Most, however, will have to be made with both legs at the same time if you hope to win a high score from the judges.

All the while, you'll be supporting and balancing yourself on your arms and hands. Only your hands will touch the horse. Sometimes you'll grip both pommels. Sometimes just one. And sometimes you'll go from pommel to pommel. The rest of your body will remain clear of the horse.

If you think that all this sounds pretty challenging, you're absolutely right. Many gymnasts feel that the side horse is just about the most difficult event that men can enter. Yet it doesn't require super strength; competitors who are on the tall and slender side seem especially good at it. What is truly required is the patience necessary to master the many different exercises.

There is just one caution that you should observe before you enter side-horse work. If you're not yet in your teens, you'll be wise to check with your coach to see if you're physically ready for the rigors ahead. While the horse doesn't require great strength, it does call for more strength than many young people yet have. Should this prove to be true in your case, then hold off a bit until the coach gives you the go-ahead nod. You'll save yourself some sore and perhaps strained muscles.

Many coaches think that the side horse shouldn't be tried until sometime in the senior high-school years.

But let's say that you're ready to start. Your first job, of course, is to get acquainted with the horse—and with the body techniques that you'll be using in your routines. This can be done by working on some basic exercises for a time. As you work, you'll need to keep three points in mind.

First, all the movements in your routines will be done in support positions—that is, you'll be leaning on your arms and hands. For the very best support positions, your arms must be kept straight. Likewise, your whole body—head, torso, and legs—should be straight, with the toes pointed. Your shoulders should never be "hunched up," but should always be held down and level so that you have the feeling of being tall.

Second, always grip the pommels tightly. Whenever you must release a pommel, never let your hand fly up in any direction. Rather, keep it under firm control and ready for its next job—perhaps to regrasp the pommel, perhaps to shoot over and grab the other pommel. The fingers should be kept together at all times and should all be pointing in the same direction.

Finally, for best balance, develop the knack of keeping your center of gravity between your hands. This is where it belongs practically every minute of the time. When you swing over onto one arm, don't shift your weight all the way over to it. Practice and experience will show you exactly how much of a shift is actually needed.

Now for the get-acquainted exercises themselves. Don't be surprised, but the first two are performed on the parallel bars rather than on the horse.

Get-acquainted Exercises

"Walking" (Picture A): This exercise will help accustom you to the support position and to shifting your weight from arm to arm. Simply move forward and backward along the parallel bars, making sure that you keep your arms straight, your legs together, and your toes pointed. To help your balance, raise your legs slightly to the front.

Later, you can switch over to the horse and "walk" along its side by moving sideways one hand at a time. All the while, keep your abdomen from touching the horse.

Body Swing (Picture B): The emphasis now is on shifting the weight from arm to arm. Support yourself between the bars, with your arms and legs straight. Shift from one arm to the other by swinging your legs from side to side. As your weight goes over on one arm, lift the opposite hand from the bar. Remember, though, don't carry your center of gravity all the way onto the support arm.

Now it's time to work on the horse itself with the *leg swing,* which is similar to the body swing. The leg swing will prepare you for the many circular and scissors movements you'll soon be attempting.

All that you do is mount the horse in the front-support position (see Picture A in the illustration on beginning mounts) and then swing your legs from side to side while you grip both pommels. When you swing to the right, send your right leg higher and higher each time. The left leg goes high on swings to the left. After a little practice, send both legs high together as you swing in one direction or the other.

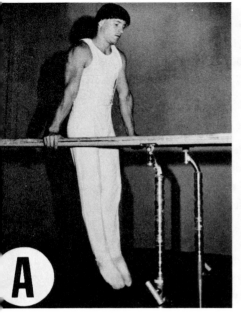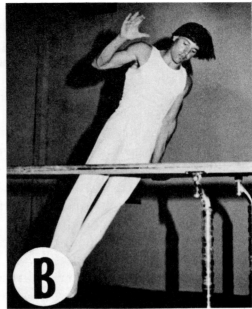

Get-acquainted Exercises: Side Horse

The leg swings should be practiced on all areas of the horse—the left and right ends, and the center section. By working all areas, you'll gain experience in a variety of hand holds. Sometimes you'll be gripping both pommels. And sometimes one hand will be on a pommel while the other is on the horse.

MOUNTS

By the time you're an experienced gymnast, you'll be able to mount the horse in several different ways, some of them quite breathtaking to watch. At the start, though, two very simple mounts will serve you well. They're called the *front-support mount* and the *half-leg-circle mount.*

Front-support Mount (Picture A): To perform this most basic of all mounts, simply stand facing the center section of the horse, with your feet togther and your hands gripping the pommels. Then jump straight up from both feet and support yourself on straight arms. You'll be in a position to start your routine with any exercise. And that's all there is to it.

Half-leg-circle Mount (Pictures B, C, and D): Now for a mount that's almost as simple—but quite a lot more fun to do and watch. Your starting position (Picture B) is at the right end of the horse. Your feet are together. Your left hand grips the right pommel. Your right hand is on the right end.

Everything begins (Picture C) when you jump up from both feet. Several actions now take place in rapid and flowing succession. Your left arm helps the jump by straightening. Your hips and legs swing out to the right. The right leg travels quite high. As the right leg rises, your right hand helps with the upward thrust by pushing itself off the horse.

When your right leg reaches the top of its swing (again Picture C), you must rotate your right hip forward. This action causes the leg to describe a tight little semicircle that carries the leg across the top of the horse. It also turns your body so that you can now swing down toward a landing.

On the downward ride, your legs close slightly so that they'll end straddling the horse. Your right hand regrasps the right end as you land (Picture D). Your right leg comes to a stop in front of the horse; your left leg is directly opposite; both are very straight. Your arms are supporting you so that your seat remains clear of the horse. To return to your starting position, all you need to do is reverse the whole procedure.

All the actions in the mount are important. But the most important one is the top-of-the-swing hip rotation that carries the right leg across the horse in a tight little semicircle. Practice steadily to master the rotation, and never allow your right leg to fly straight out across the horse. Only with the little semicircle are you able to turn easily and enter a graceful downward flight.

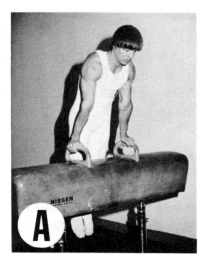

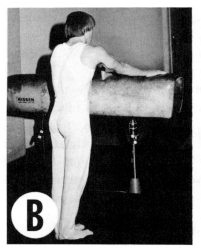

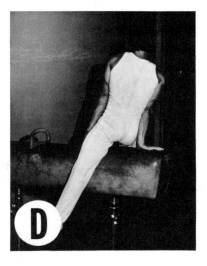

Two Beginning Mounts

After you've practiced the mount for a time, you should vary things by moving to the left end and sending your left leg high in the jump. Very soon—along with all good gymnasts—you'll be able to mount the horse from either end with equal ease.

MOVEMENTS

Once you're up on the horse, you're ready for some competition movements. Here are four that can be used in your first routine. We'll start with circles made with one leg and then move on to one using both legs together.

Single-leg Half Circle (Pictures A and B): This movement is similar to the half-circle mount. The chief difference is that it is launched from the front-support position on the center section. Your back is straight, and each hand grasps a pommel.

Begin by shifting your weight to the left and swinging your hips and legs to the right. Send your right leg quite high (Picture A).

At the top of the swing, thrust your right hand up from the pommel and rotate your hip forward. Let your right leg ride across the horse and sweep downward. The leg passes between your upraised right hand and the right pommel. Everything ends (Picture B) when you regrasp the pommel and come to a stop with your legs straddling the center section.

Why is this movement—and the mount of a moment ago—called a half-circle exercise? Because your right leg is actually cutting a circular path as it crosses the top of the horse and swings downward. You keep the leg from completely circling the horse by stopping midway when you reach the center section.

Single-leg Full Circle (Picture C): To perform a full circle, begin just as if you're planning the half circle. Legs and hips swing to the right from the front-support position. The right leg shoots high, crosses the horse, and descends. You straddle the center section.

But things don't end at this point. Rather, as indicated in Picture C, your right leg continues its swing, now heading for the left end of the

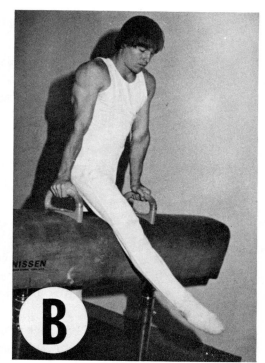

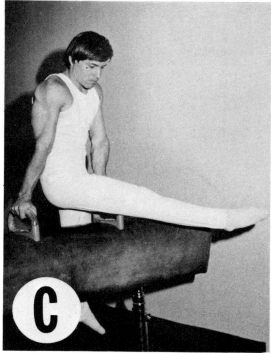

Single-leg Half and Full Circles

horse. Your left hand pulls up from the left pommel, and your travel-ing leg passes through the open space between the two as it crosses to the rear of the horse. Back to the pommel goes your hand once the leg is safely past. You'll find yourself once more in your original front-support position.

Half-leg-circle Travel

A movement that carries you from one area of the horse to another is called a *travel*. For a beginning journey, let's say that you've just gotten up on the horse with the half-circle mount. You're straddling the right end (Picture A) and planning to move to the center section.

As you complete the mount, carry your left leg forward so that (Picture B) it rides across the center section and drops in alongside the right pommel. Next (Picture C), thrust your right hand up from the right end and send your right leg back through the open space to the rear of the horse.

So far so good. Now, one after the other, come two actions. First (Picture D), bring your right hand over to join your left in gripping the pommel. Second, immediately swing your left leg across to the rear of the horse. And (Picture E) there you are—in a front-support position on the center section, having "traveled" there from the right end.

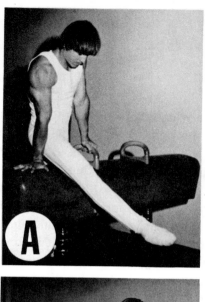

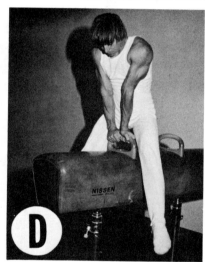

The Half-leg-circle Travel

Right Feint

Feints are circular movements in which the hands do not leave the pommels. Feints may be made to the right or left, and with just one leg or both legs together. One of the simplest of all—the *right feint*—begins in the front-support position on the center section.

The feint is done by first shifting your weight to the right arm and then swinging your right leg across the horse, much as if you're performing a half circle. This time, however, your right hand doesn't leave the pommel. As pictured, the movement ends with your legs straddling your right arm as it extends straight up from the pommel.

The right feint is often used to gather momentum for dismounts or for more advanced stunts. The momentum develops when you swing out of the feint position and carry your legs back behind the horse. We'll now see this momentum at work as we turn to the skill of dismounting.

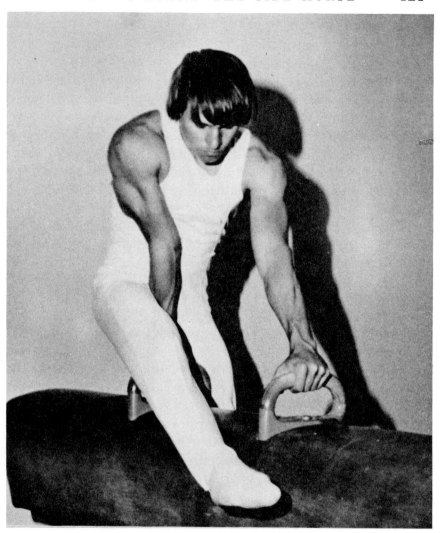

The Right Feint

DISMOUNT

As is true of the mounts, there are various ways to dismount the horse. They range, of course, from the simple to the complex. All dismounts require that you land on the balls of your feet and dip your knees to absorb the impact. One hand usually rests on the horse and the other is gracefully extended out to the side or upward. As soon as you land, you should drop down from the balls of your feet, straighten your legs, lower your hands to your sides, and come to attention.

Now let's put the right feint to work in a dismount that some coaches say is a beginning one; others say it belongs in the intermediate category. It's called the *single rear dismount*.

Single Rear Dismount

All right. There you are (Picture A) in the right-feint position. To gather momentum for the dismount, swing your right leg back over the horse.

Once the right leg is to the rear of the horse, bring it alongside your left leg. Swing them both forward (Picture B) so that they arc upward and pass across the left end. As they rise, pull your left hand clear of the left pommel. Your legs ride through the open space and down you come (Picture C) in front of the horse to a landing on both feet, with your right hand extended out to the side. Please note your left hand. It's back holding the left pommel. It returns to the pommel as you drop to the landing.

The feint that gives you the momentum for the dismount should be practiced from both the right and the left ends. Then the dismount itself can be done from either the left or the right, thus giving you two separate ways of leaving the horse.

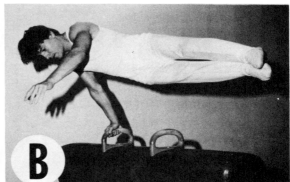

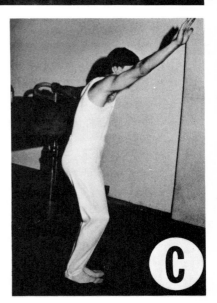

The Single Rear Dismount

7 A Men's Event—
The Parallel Bars

The parallel bars were developed by the father of modern gymnastics, Friedrich Jahn of Germany, in the early nineteenth century. He intended at first that the students in his gymnasium would use them as a preparation for side-horse work. The bars, however, proved so popular that they soon grew into a separate event.

Both men and women competed on the parallel bars until well into our own century. Then the women moved over to the uneven parallel bars. There they could perform stunts more suitable to their builds—stunts that didn't require so much strength and that put the accent on grace and suppleness.

Though strictly a men's event today, the parallel bars are said to be closer to the women's balance beam than to the side horse or the rings. Why? Because both the beam and the bars happily accept a great many skills learned in other events. Are you, for instance, good at rolls or presses in floor exercise? How about circling movements on the side horse? Or swinging movements on the rings? They can all be transferred to the bars with a little practice.

Indeed, because you can perform so many stunts on the bars, many gymnasts see them as the most varied of the men's events.

THE PARALLEL BARS

Just as the name indicates, the equipment consists of two bars running side by side above the floor. Each is round and made of wood.

They're supported near each end by metal uprights that are fastened to a base to hold the entire apparatus in place as you perform.

The bars are 11½ feet long. So far as height is concerned, they can usually be adjusted from a low of 3 feet, 9 inches to a high of 5 feet, 9 inches. The lower heights are using during practice sessions. In competition, the heights generally run from 5 feet, 7 inches to 5 feet, 9 inches.

The distance between the bars is also adjustable. The adjustment is needed so that gymnasts of different sizes can compete comfortably. Ordinarily, the widths run from 19 to 25 inches for competitions involving full-grown gymnasts. But it can be narrowed to 14 or 15 inches for younger competitors.

GETTING STARTED

Though all sorts of movements can be performed on the bars, they are usually divided into two categories. The categories are the same as those for the rings: *swinging parts* and *hold positions*. Hold positions include strength movements—such as the press to a handstand —and the swinging parts include tumbling stunts.

When you begin to build a competitive routine, you'll find that it will have to be made up mostly of swinging parts. Also, as is true of other events, all the movements will have to flow smoothly from one to another. In fact, you'll be permitted to include no more than three hold positions. Hold positions, of course, bring you to a stop. No stop may last more than one second. Stops of two or more seconds will damage your score.

And, as you prepare your routine, you'll find that practically every swinging movement requires you to release the bars with one hand or the other at some point along the way. In the next instant, you must regrasp the bars. The continual actions of releasing and regrasping will sharpen your senses of timing and balance to the finest edge possible.

In addition, the bars will develop your agility and flexibility. Physically, your upper torso—especially the arms and shoulders—will be greatly strengthened.

The manner in which you carry your body is all-important in bars work. Always strive to be as "tall" as possible, fully extending the body on swings, handstands, and such. And be sure to pay close attention to your back. It should always be as straight as you can make it. You'll need to arch it at times, but try to keep the arches slight. A "tall" body will help to carry you gracefully through all the stunts in a routine; a deeply arched back will tire you very quickly.

Get-acquainted Exercises

Before attempting to learn any of the competitive movements themselves, you'll need to acquaint yourself with the arm positions basic to all bars work. They're all support positions, with the arms straight at times and bent at others. The following exercises will introduce you to them and will also help you to build the arm and shoulder strength necessary for a solid performance.

They—and all the stunts that follow—should be first practiced on a set of low bars if at all possible. There will be less risk of a nasty fall if you'll gather a little skill and confidence before testing any new movement at competition height.

Straight-arm Support Mount (Pictures A and B): Actually, this is a mount that you may use in competition if you wish. It's included here in the get-acquainted section so that you won't have to scramble up on the bars in any old way for the exercises. Also, because it involves entering and holding the first of the basic arm positions, it's a valuable exercise on its own.

Stand at the extreme end of the bars, with your back straight and your feet together. Let yourself stand close enough so that your elbows are comfortably bent as you grasp the bars in the *overgrip*— knuckles on top and thumbs underneath. Launch the mount (Picture A) with a bend of the knees and jump straight up. Help yourself along by thrusting down on your hands and then straightening your arms as you rise above the bars.

End (Picture B) in the straight-arm support, with the head high, and the back and legs straight. Hold the position for several counts, familiarizing yourself with it. You're going to be using it before, during, and after all sorts of stunts as you become an experienced gymnast.

Straight-arm Swing (Picture C): Once you're supporting yourself on straight arms, launch a series of swings by pumping your legs backward and forward. Concentrate on keeping your arms straight all the while and on making the swings from the shoulders. If you're to swing freely and easily through future stunts, you must early establish

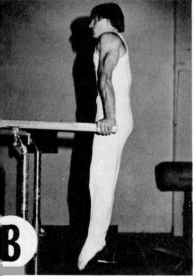

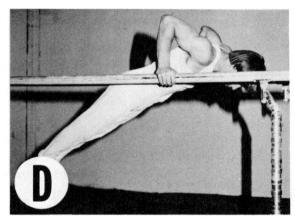

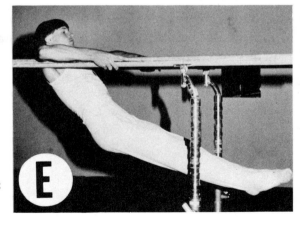

**Parallel Bars:
Get-acquainted Exercises**

the habit of doing so from the shoulders. You may help matters by imagining yourself to be a lever connected to shoulders that are a fulcrum.

Start with low swings. Gradually increase the arcs as the days go by until, as seen in the picture, your body is rising well above the bars.

After a time, begin to push your hands against the bars at the end of each backswing. This will cause the hands to jump slightly. You'll gain some beginning experience in releasing and regrasping the bars.

Dip (Picture D): This is the second of the basic arm positions, one in which you support yourself on deeply bent arms. As you drop into the position from the straight-arm support, you'll need to do three things. First, bring your shoulders well ahead of your elbows. Second, bend the elbows just beyond a ninety-degree angle. And third, aim the forearms as straight up from the bars as you can.

You can increase your arm and shoulder strength by performing several dips at a time each day. Drop down from the straight-arm support, hold each dip for a few counts, and then return to the straight-arm support. Of course, to avoid sore muscles, start with just a few.

Then—and this really adds to the fun—try some *swinging dips.* Start with a backward swing from the straight-arm support position. At the end of the swing, bend the arms so that you now swing forward in the dip position. Thrust back up to the straight-arm support at the end of the forward swing.

Upper-arm Support (Picture E): Here's a support position that brings you right down to the bars. From the straight-arm position, drop slowly with a deep elbow bend until you're riding on your upper arms. The elbows are out to the side. Your hands are directly ahead, holding the bars.

Once in the upper-arm support, practice swinging back and forth. Again, let the swings come from the shoulders. Remember to think of yourself as a lever and of your shoulders as a fulcrum.

MOUNTING THE BARS

We've already tried the most basic of the many ways to mount the bars. Let's turn now to a method that's far more exciting—exciting because it contains a leg-and-arm movement similar to one that you learned up on the rings. Its name: the *single-leg cut-on mount*.

Stand holding the ends of the bars (Picture A) just as you did when preparing to launch the straight-arm mount. Then, as before, jump straight up. Push your hands down on the bars and straighten your arms to help yourself along. . . .

Now comes the action that is similar to the one on the rings. As you rise, hold your right leg steady and send it between the bars. But angle your left leg out to the side so that it passes on the outside of the left bar. What you're about to do is swing the leg over the top of the bar and drop it to the inside. Clear a path (Picture B) by pulling your left hand up from the bar. Send the leg through the open space and immediately regrasp the bar. End (Picture C) in the straight-arm support between the bars.

For safety's sake, the mount should be practiced just one step at a time on a set of low bars. Do no more at the start than practice sending the left leg wide on the jump; drop straight back down at the end of each try. Next, practice the hand release and over-the-bar swing; don't try to regrasp the bar after the swing, but simply land on your feet between the bars. Once you're thoroughly accustomed to the release and swing, add the regrasp and finish in the straight-arm position.

The mount can also be performed with an outward swing of the right leg. Then, as you become a more skilled gymnast, you'll be able to vary things to a double-leg cut-off. Now both legs ride out to the side. Up goes one hand. The legs travel through the open space together and drop between the bars.

The Single-leg Cut-on Mount

SWINGING MOVEMENTS

Swinging movements can be performed from any of the basic support positions that we've practiced. Here are some beginning swings from each of the three supports.

Straight-arm Swings

Forward Swing to Straddle Seat (Pictures A and B): Nothing could be easier to do than this one. From the straight-arm support, swing your legs forward above the bars. Separate the legs (Picture A) as soon as they clear the bars. Then let them drop (Picture B) so that you sit straddling the bars.

At the close of the movement, your back should be straight, your head high, your chest up, and your hands directly behind your legs.

Straddle-seat Travel (Pictures C, D, and E): Various movements can be triggered from the straddle-seat position. To enter one of the most basic of the lot, lean forward (Picture C) and grasp the bars a few inches in front of your thighs. Then (Picture D) swing your legs back and up. Let them ride down between the bars and rise high to the front. Separate them at the end of the forward swing. End again (Picture E) in the straddle seat. You may travel forward the length of the bars with repeats of the swing. Reverse the procedure to move backward.

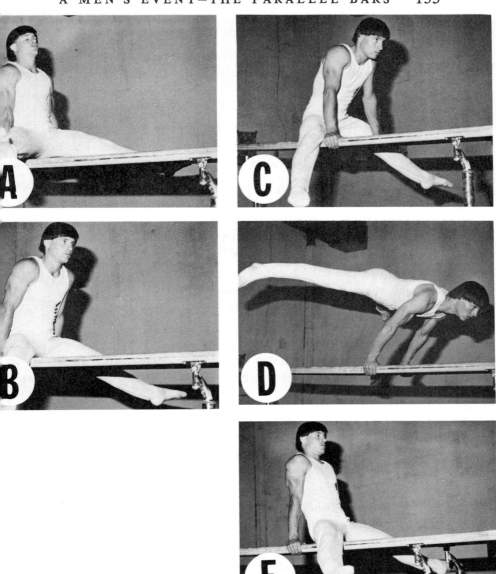

Straight-arm Swings

Straight-arm Swing and Turn

If you're to travel back and forth along the bars, you'll need to turn about while swinging. Every routine is dotted with a variety of turning movements. Let's try the following one for a start. It's called the *straight-arm turn*.

You'll likely think that you're back swinging on the side horse whenever you perform this basic two-part movement. The first part begins when you break out of the straight-arm support by leaning to your right. Pull your left hand up from its bar. Swing your body about (Picture A) and bring the front of your thighs against the right bar. Now over comes your left hand to grasp the right bar.

For the second part of the turn (Picture B), pull the right hand away and send it over to the left bar. At the same time, swing your body in pursuit of the hand. You'll end facing in the opposite direction and back in the straight-arm support.

The turn can be made to the left by reversing the procedure.

A Dipped-arm Swing

An energetic movement can be tried as soon as you've mastered the swinging dip in the get-acquainted exercises. It's called the *swinging-dip travel*.

To perform the movement, start with a backward swing while in the straight-arm position. Lower yourself to the dip as the legs swing forward. Then, at the top of the forward swing, push your hands down hard against the bars, straighten your arms, and thrust yourself forward.

Your hands will leave the bars for an instant and send you "hopping" forward a few inches. Continue the "hops" by dipping again and then thrusting upward and ahead at the top of the next forward swing.

If you wish to hop backward, save the upward thrust for the end of the backswing.

Straight-arm Swing and Turn

An Upper-arm Swing

The first upper-arm swing learned by beginners is the *back uprise.* It requires a high upward swing at the start and then a strong arm movement to send you into the position that ends the movement.

As soon as you've dropped into the upper-arm-support position at the end of some movement, swing your legs back and forth to gain momentum. On a forward swing (Picture A), carry them high overhead in a pike position. Then (Picture B) whip them back down and into a strong backswing. Your arm strength comes into play at the top of the backswing. Pull hard on your arms and straighten them, thrusting upward at the same time (Picture B) so that your body—well extended—angles high above the bars. Keep the body fully extended as you swing downward to end in a straight-arm support.

The upward thrust at the top of the backswing is known as a *cast.* You'll find it further explained in chapter 4, where it's used several times on the women's uneven parallel bars.

The Back Uprise

HOLD POSITIONS

Though you're permitted only three hold positions in a routine, they can be among the most breathtaking stunts you'll ever perform. To see just how breathtaking, you need only watch a gymnast press into a handstand and, with his body pointing straight up from the bars, release one hand and remain balanced on the other.

But it will be quite a while before you're ready to make an audience gasp with that stunt. Yet, even while you're still a beginner, you can cause plenty of excitement with a hold position that requires a combination of good balance and solid strength. It's called the *shoulder stand*.

The movement begins while you're in the straddle-seat position. Grasping the bars a few inches in front of the thighs (Picture A), lean forward and lift the hips into the air. The lift will bring your straddled legs clear of the bar and leave you balancing on bent arms for a brief moment. When you feel the weight on your arms, turn your bent elbows outward. Let your upper arms drop to the bars (Picture B). Your weight will automatically transfer to them.

Continue raising your hips as your upper arms drop to the bar. Once the upper arms are in position, bring your legs together. Finish everything off by raising the legs until (Picture C) they're straight overhead. When you're finally in the shoulder stand, your back should be as straight as possible. Point your toes straight at the ceiling.

You may drop out of the shoulder stand in either of two ways. First, you may reverse the procedure and return to your starting position. Or you may roll forward to a straddle seat. This is done by piking the legs and carrying the hips forward and down so that you travel across your shoulders and then along your back. As you're moving along your back, separate your legs so that they'll straddle the bars when you rise to a sitting position at the end.

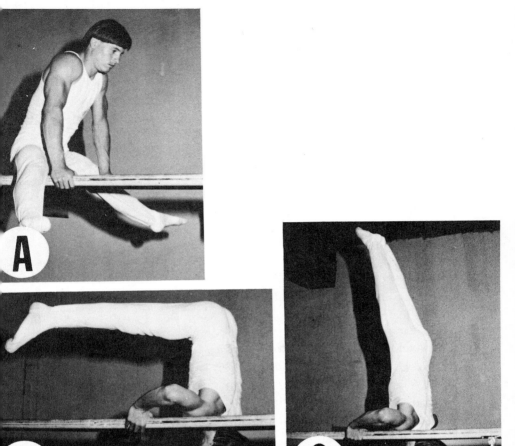

The Shoulder Stand

TUMBLING ON THE BARS

The shoulder stand and the roll that brings you down from it are tumbling movements that have been transferred from floor exercises to the bars. If you'd like to "tumble" some more, here are two stunts that will add much to any beginning routine.

Forward Roll (Picture A): Starting in the straddle-seat position, grasp the bars a comfortable distance in front of your thighs. Lean forward, place the upper arms on the bars, and bend the elbows out to the side. Simultaneously, carry the hips up and forward until they pass overhead.

As soon as the hips are overhead (Picture A), release the bars and move your hands forward, regrasping the bars just ahead of your back. Continue the roll until you're once more in the straddle-seat position.

Backward Roll (Pictures B and C): Start again from the straddle seat. But this time, reach behind you to grasp the bars. Then (Picture B), piking the body, roll along your back until your hips pass overhead. Release the bars (Picture C) and regrasp them several inches to the front of your head. Continue rolling. End in the straddle position.

A Different Ending (Picture D): If you wish, you need not conclude either roll in the straddle position. Rather, keeping the legs together, you may drop between the bars in the upper-arm support.

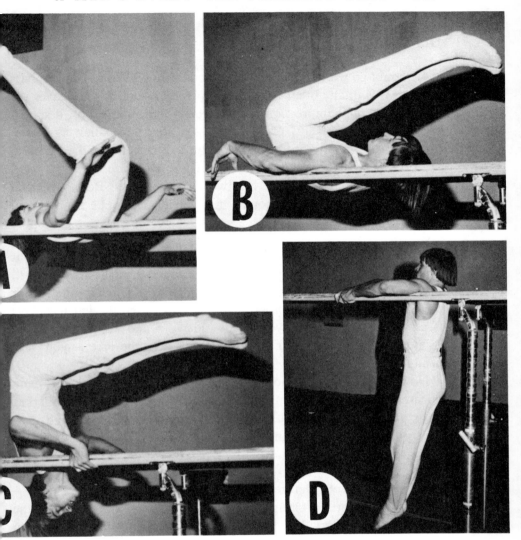

Forward and Backward Rolls

DISMOUNTS

It should go without saying that a good dismount is as vital in bars work as it is in any other event. It "caps off" a routine and leaves the judges with a fine impression of your work. To do these jobs, it should contain all the elements of any successful dismount—flowing movement, a neat landing on the balls of the feet, a bend of the knees to absorb the impact, and an immediate snap to attention.

To close the chapter, here are two fine dismounts. Both will open the way to the exciting dismounts that you'll one day be trying as an expert gymnast.

Rear Dismount (Pictures A and B): This simplest of dismounts is similar to a vault over your back fence. From a straight-arm support, pike the body and send the legs over the right bar. As the legs clear the bar (Picture A), push your left hand away from the left bar. This is an action that thrusts your body sideways and sends it over the right bar in pursuit of your legs. Straighten from the pike as your legs head for the floor.

Now comes a final movement of the hands. Your right hand releases the right bar, and your left hand travels over to grasp the bar in its place. You drop to a landing (Picture B) outside the right bar, with your left hand holding the bar, and your right hand extended outward.

Front Dismount (Pictures C and D): The front dismount looks— and is—far more exciting to perform. It, too, begins from the straight-arm support, but with a strong forward swing. The swing must be strong so that it provides you with the momentum to whip into a backswing that carries your body above the bars in a cast.

At the top of the cast, there's a rapid movement of the hands. First, thrust your left hand forcefully up from the left bar so that it pushes your body to the outside of the right bar. Bring the left hand over to grasp the right bar. Release the right hand (Picture C) and send it out to the side.

Front and Rear Dismounts

Then finish off (Picture D) by arcing down to a landing, with your left hand holding the right bar.

Both dismounts can send you to the left of the bars as well as to the right. As usual, reverse the procedure if you wish to travel to the left.

8 A Men's Event— The Horizontal Bar

Many gymnasts think that the side horse is the most difficult of the men's events. Some look on the parallel bars as the most varied event, and the still rings as the one demanding the greatest strength. But everyone agrees on one point: The horizontal bar takes first prize as the most spectacular event.

There are two reasons for the honor. First, often stretched out full length, the gymnast goes whipping around the bar time and again, never stopping, but turning his body and switching directions as he goes. Second, his dismounts have the habit of leaving the spectators speechless. It's common for him to sail more than twelve feet into the air before dropping to a landing.

We can thank Friedrich Jahn for this most spectacular of events. The bar is another of his early-nineteenth-century inventions, with the idea for it coming to him while he was watching some children swing from the limbs of a tree. Right from the beginning, he felt that work on the bar would develop courage and daring, and would build fine strength in the shoulders and arms. Anyone who has competed on the bar will tell you that Jahn was absolutely right.

THE HORIZONTAL BAR

Supported by metal uprights at either end, the horizontal bar measures just over eight feet long. Its height is 8 feet, 2½ inches. The metal uprights may stand on a base or be inserted into the floor. Steel cables, stretched taut, hold the uprights steady.

The bar itself is round, with a diameter of just over 1 inch. Though it started life as an outsized piece of wooden doweling, the bar is now made of solid spring steel. It's very flexible and will easily bend up to four inches or so with each movement made by a gymnast of average weight. It pops back straight as soon as it's released.

Gymnasts appreciate the flexibility in a good-quality bar. It actually assists them in traveling through their various swinging movements. A "stiff" bar will slow you down and tire you quickly.

Though there is only one height used in competition, most horizontal bars are adjustable. They are brought down to shoulder or head height for practice purposes.

GETTING STARTED

When you begin to swing on the horizontal bar, you're going to find that a great deal of stress is immediately put on your hands—not to mention all the friction of the steel rubbing against your palms. The fact is, you're going to find that, of all the events for men, the bar is the toughest one on the hands.

Right from the start, you'll need to do all that you can to protect your hands against blistering and tearing. In time, you'll build a set of tough calluses that will serve as fine safeguards.

Actually, there are three things you can do for protection. First, don't hesitate to use plenty of gymnastic chalk. Or wear handguards. Some coaches think that you shouldn't be given a choice about handguards. They say that anyone who gets up on the bar should be required to wear them.

Second, don't try to work for long periods when first practicing. Short stints will, of course, give the hands less of a chance to blister or tear. And be aware of the hands as you practice. If you feel them starting to grow sore, stop for a while—or even for the day, and let them recover.

Finally try to avoid a problem common to practically all beginners. Concentrate on not gripping the bar too tightly. Develop the habit of cupping the hands around the bar rather than squeezing it. This technique, which keeps the skin from dragging against the bar or "bunching up" in the fleshy area below the fingers as you swing, may seem a difficult one to learn. But you'll soon acquire the knack if you'll keep the idea of "cupping" always in mind.

One more thought: As you and your friends practice, a great deal of chalk is going to build up on the bar. In excess, chalk may irritate some hands; and it will usually keep you from getting a secure grip on the bar. Make sure that you clean it away periodically with steel wool, sandpaper, or emery paper. But don't clean every last bit away, for then the bar may feel slippery.

All beginning work should be done on a bar that has been lowered to chest or head height. It doesn't take much imagination to know that a fall from eight feet can hurt, and so you'll work with greater confidence—and, as a result, advance more quickly—at a lower "altitude." Also, your spotters can be of greater help if you're down within easy reach. Raise the bar gradually as your skill increases. You'll soon be up to competition height.

A competitive routine is composed of two basic kinds of stunts—*supports* and *hanging movements*. The supports, of course, send you up on your arms, just as they do on the side horse and parallel bars. The hanging movements include all the great swings that make the horizontal bar such a breathtaking event.

Every routine must contain a variety of stunts, including some in which you change direction by turning the body, and some in which both hands leave the bar. All the stunts must be performed smoothly and without stopping. Any stops at all—even hesitations—are considered poor form and will damage your score.

There are many movements possible for use in a routine. In fact, it has long been said that the number of possibilities is almost infinite because movements can be changed into new ones simply by altering the position of your body or the manner in which your hands grip the bar. Thanks to all this, gymnasts usually find it difficult to build a routine. The problem is to pick just the right movements for you from all that are available.

But this is a problem that needn't worry you just yet. Your first job is to get up on the horizontal bar and learn the basic skills that it demands of every gymnast. Once you're well on your way to mastering them, then it will be time to start thinking about entering competitions.

SUPPORT MOVEMENTS

For convenience and safety, let's start with some support movements. They can be practiced with the bar at a lower level than is possible for swings.

As you've done in all events, patiently learn and practice the movements individually. Then begin to combine them for your first "feel" of what it will be like to do a competitive routine. So that you'll never damage a future score with hesitations, work for the day when you can perform each movement—and then each combination—without stopping.

Here, to start things, is a simple support position that should be more than familiar to you by now.

The Front Support

This position is used at the beginning and at the end of many support movements. It looks just as it does on the side horse and parallel bars: You're up on vertical arms, with your back straight, your legs together, and your toes pointed floorward.

With the bar set low for practice, you can mount to the front support in basically the same way as before. Simply stand facing one side of the bar (either side will do—it's your choice), extend your arms directly ahead, and take the bar in the *regular grip*. The fingers curve over the top of the bar, and the thumb is against the underside.

As usual, bend your knees and jump upward. And, as usual, end with your arms supporting your weight. Your hips should be resting against the bar.

Now let's try some movements in which the front support plays a part.

The Front Support: Horizontal Bar

Hip Pullover and Circles

Hip Pullover (Pictures A and B): Stand facing one side of the bar, again with your arms forward and your hands in the regular grip. Begin by pulling your chest toward the bar and jumping forward. In the same instant, pike your body so that your legs swing forward beneath the bar.

By pulling your midsection up to the bar (Picture A), send your legs, still piked, up the far side of the bar. Carry them across the top of the bar. Follow with your torso until it, too, passes above the bar. Then, as your legs are heading back down toward the floor, straighten your body (Picture B) and end in the front-support position.

After some practice, raise the bar and try the pullover from a long hang—that is, while hanging full length. Since you're starting from a stationary position, you'll need to gather momentum with a few swings and then pike your body on a strong forward swing. Though all right here, the extra swings would be frowned on in competition; but, of course, you won't need them at that time because you'll be entering the pullover from some other stunt and will have ample momentum going for you.

Hip Circle Backward (Pictures C and D): Once you're in the front-support position, swing your legs forward slightly to gain momentum. Then carry them backward. At the top of the backswing (Picture C), thrust up from the bar in the *cast* that you learned on the parallel bars.

Now let the legs ride forward, keeping them together. When your abdomen strikes the bar (Picture D), pike the body and send the legs up the far side. Pull with your arms so that you continue circling until you return to the front-support position.

Hip Circle Forward (Picture E): For this one, as you prepare to leave the front-support position, elevate your chest and extend your body out as straight as you can. With the chest leading (Picture E), ride forward until you pass through the point where your body is horizontal to the floor.

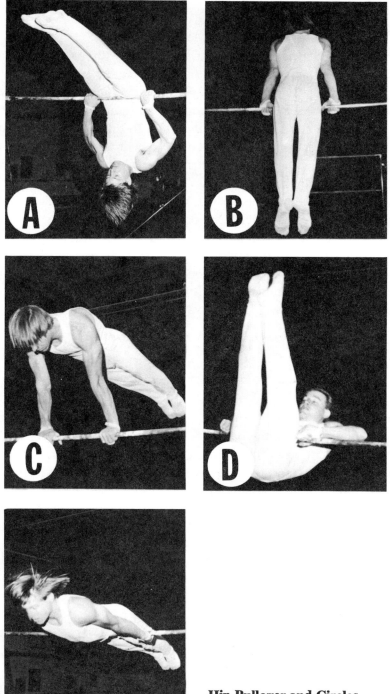

Hip Pullover and Circles

On passing the horizontal point, pull hard with your hands, and whip your head and chest beneath the bar. Pike the legs as you do so. Keeping your hips against the bar, continue circling. When you reach the top of the bar, enter the front-support position.

The position of the chest is all-important to the movement. Be sure to keep the chest well forward, letting it lead the way through the whole circle. Leading, it will contribute to your momentum. If you pull it back, it will slow you down.

When you think the time is right, raise the bar for your first experiments at a higher "altitude." One caution, however: Many gymnasts find the hip circles—especially the forward one—rather difficult to perform. If you suspect that you're going to have trouble with them, you'll be wise to save them until you try the movements that now follow. The following stunts are a little easier to do. They'll give you some experience that will later prove helpful.

Single-leg Swing-up and Circles

These support movements are performed while one leg or the other is hooked over the bar.

Single-leg Swing-up (Pictures A, B, and C): The movement begins as you're hanging from the bar, with one leg—in this instance, the left —tucked up between your arms and hooked over the bar. The right leg is extended out parallel to the floor below.

Gather momentum (Picture A) by swinging the right leg upward. Then (Picture B) whip it downward, keeping it perfectly straight as you do so. Pull with the arms at the same time and work the hands up toward the top of the bar. You'll swing upward until (Picture C) you're on top of the bar and in the *single-knee-support position*. The left leg is still resting on the bar at the knee, and the right leg is extended to the rear.

Following some practice, raise the bar and try the movement from a long hang. Start by swinging back and forth to gather momentum. On a forward swing, kick the left leg high, send it between your arms, and hook it over the bar, after which the stunt is completed as before.

Starting as you are from a stationary position, it's all right to gather

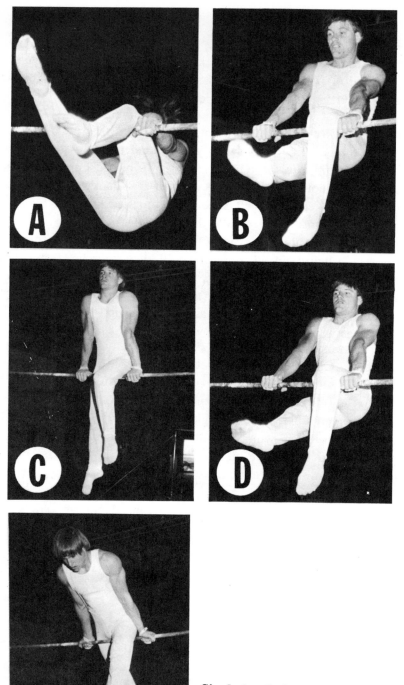

Single-leg Swing-up and Circles

some additional momentum by kicking the left leg two or three times before sending it between the arms. But remember: Along with extra swings, the kicks won't do in competition.

Single-leg Circle Backward (Picture D): From the single-knee support atop the bar, forcefully swing your extended right leg downward. At the same time, push your torso away from the bar with a little thrust of the shoulders. Then let yourself fall backward. Circle beneath the bar. Keep your left knee firmly hooked over the bar. Continue the circle until you return to the top of the bar.

Plenty of momentum is needed to get you completely through the circle. You'll help yourself along if you'll keep your head and shoulders thrown well back at all times; in this manner, they'll actually be leading the way and contributing to your momentum. Then, as you approach the top of the bar, a strong pull with the arms will be needed to assist you the rest of the way up.

Single-leg Circle Forward (Picture E): You must change your hold on the bar to the *reverse grip* for this movement. Place your thumb to the front of the bar and the fingers to the rear.

Push yourself up from the single-knee-support position and whip yourself forward. With your head and chest leading all the while, pass beneath the bar and come up the far side, returning at last to your original position. Throughout the circle, help yourself along by moving your hands forward.

It's as important here to lead with your head and shoulders as it was to lead with them on the circle backward. If you pull them back, you'll hinder your momentum.

HANGING MOVEMENTS

When you're ready to try your first swings, raise the bar until you can hang from it full length without having the toes touch the floor when they're pointed downward. Your work should then begin with the *free swing*.

Free Swing

The free swing is the most important of all the basic movements. You're going to be using it constantly for as long as you perform on the bar—to enter stunts, to ride through them, to exit from them, and to join them together. In time, you'll be using it to send you on your way through dazzling swings that will carry you, with body fully extended, completely around the bar.

From the moment that you jump up to a long hang for your first practice session, keep one thought uppermost in mind: Always try to make the swing look smooth, relaxed, and skillful. It will then make your whole routine look smooth, relaxed, and skillful.

Once you're hanging full length from the bar by means of the regular grip, break out of the stationary position by swinging your legs up to the front and then arcing them downward and to the rear. As you come forward again, pump the legs slightly. To increase your height, pump again on each forward swing.

The pumping action should take place just a second or so after you come forward under the bar. It will take a little experience for you to determine the exact moment for the action.

Except when pumping, the body should be in a straight line from the extended arms right down to the toes. The hips are bound to fall a little behind on each pump. But once the pump is completed, they should be moved upward and forward so that they're in line once again.

Remember to cup the bar with your hands rather than squeeze it. Your wrists should bend on the front swings. The bar should slide in your hands on the backswings.

A good free swing can be pretty exhilarating, especially when you're rising through an arc that's carrying you higher and higher each time. But don't let yourself be carried away into exceptionally high swings. Limit the arc of each swing between the tops at the front and back to 45 to 180 degrees. Should you rise too high, you'll risk losing your grip and ending up sprawled on the mat below.

Later, when you become a skilled gymnast who knows how to adjust his handgrips, you'll be able to travel through all sorts of high swings.

The Free Swing

Swings and Turns

As was said earlier, swings can be multiplied into an almost endless number of stunts by changing your body position or the grip of your hands. To start you on your way to mastering as many of these stunts as you can, here's a very basic turning movement. It's known as a *swinging half turn left—one-hand release.*

Begin by launching a free swing. Pump your legs to gain height. Then, as you're approaching the top of a front swing with your body extended in a straight line, turn your head and shoulders to the left. At the same time (Picture A), release your right hand. Pull it away from the bar, send it across your left hand, and regrasp the bar in the regular grip at a point just beyond. Complete the turn of your body (Picture B) so that, as you swing downward, you're facing the front.

Please note the hands (Picture C). Each is holding the bar in the regular grip. But the knuckles of your left hand are beneath the bar. Thanks to your turning action, the knuckles of the right hand are above the bar and aimed in the direction of the swing you're now entering. The hands are in what is called the *mixed grip.*

The swinging half turn is an easy movement to perform. Pay attention to your legs, though, for they may have a tendency to fly apart as you make the turn. It's a common problem for beginners and should be corrected immediately.

Also, to cut down on the possibility of a tumble, you should spend some time practicing the hand movement before actually trying the swing. Simply hang in a stationary position and shift the right hand back and forth between its old position and its new position, turning your head and shoulders as you do so.

The swinging half turn can be made in the opposite direction by sending the left hand over to a point just beyond the right.

As you become an accomplished gymnast, you'll be able to execute the half turns by releasing both hands simultaneously. Your body will turn while your hands hang suspended above the bar for a split second. Then, together, the hands will regrasp the bar.

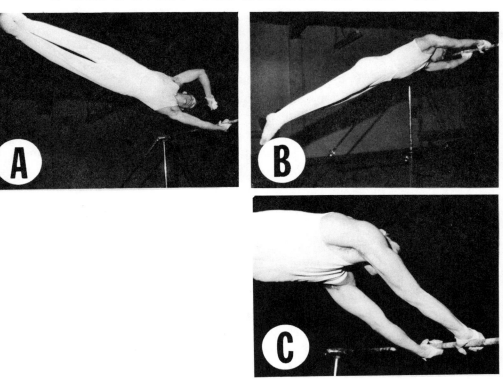

Swinging Half Turn Left—One-hand Release

MOUNTING AND DISMOUNTING

There is nothing very spectacular about the way you'll mount the bar in competition. Simply approach it from either direction and jump straight up to a long hang.

As soon as you catch the bar, you'll need to pump your legs slightly to start the initial swing that prepares you for your first movement. This initial swing is not a full free swing. Its sole purpose is to give you the momentum necessary to enter your opening stunt, and so it may not carry you back and forth more than once. Any additional arcs will see your score damaged.

But, as was said at the beginning of the chapter, dismounts from the horizontal bar can leave everyone gasping. Most of the time, the gymnast flies high before coming in for a landing. These high flights, however, cannot be attempted until you've acquired quite a bit of skill and confidence. The following two will serve you well for a start.

The simplest of all dismounts is made by dropping from the bar during a free swing. The drop should come at the top of a backswing —in that split second of dead time. With your momentum suspended momentarily, you'll be able to drop vertically to the floor. Land just as you would in any other event—on the balls of the feet, with your arms outstretched gracefully for balance, and with a bend of the knees to cushion the impact. Drop your heels immediately and come smartly to attention.

For a more exciting way of leaving the bar, let's try the *underswing dismount*.

The dismount can be easily launched from the front-support position (Picture A). Start by swinging the legs forward beneath the bar and letting the torso ride down and backward. On dropping below the bar at the end of straight arms (Picture B), pike the body and shoot the legs up the far side of the bar. Then whip them forward (Picture C), stretching yourself out to your full length as you do so. As you shoot forward, arch the back strongly. Now release the bar and arc downward to a landing (Picture D).

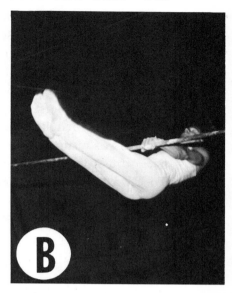

The Underswing Dismount

The dismount should first be practiced with the bar set low, at about shoulder height. Here you need not enter the front support. Holding the bar at arms' length in the regular grip, swing one leg up high beneath the bar and lean far backward. Immediately follow with the other leg, pike the body, and send them both up the far side. Then, pulling yourself up close to the bar, fire the legs forward, stretch out with arched back, release the bar, and land.

Once you're up on the high bar, the action of dropping the torso backward from the front-support position may frighten you a little. To accustom yourself to the action, just drop backward and into a long hang several times. Then add the body pike. And finally—all together—the forward thrust, the full extension, and the release.

9 For Everyone—Vaulting

Vaulting differs from most other events because it is open to both men and women. And it differs from *all* other events because it does not require the performance of a routine. Instead, it consists of just one stunt—a leap that carries the gymnast above a vaulting horse.

Altogether, the vault takes no more than a few seconds to complete. But whether you're a man or a woman, it's a real thrill. You come running along the gym floor to catapult yourself up and over the horse. Your hands touch the horse as you fly above it. They thrust you into the main part of the vault—a flight that may see you cartwheeling, somersaulting, or twisting in one direction or another before dropping to a landing.

There's all the excitement that you could want in those few seconds. And plenty of fun. In fact, many young people feel that vaulting is *the* "fun" event in gymnastics. Often, they say, you have to develop a liking for the other events. But vaulting is a good time right from the start.

VAULTING

Two pieces of equipment are used in vaulting—the vaulting horse itself and a beatboard.

The horse is nothing more than Friedrich Jahn's side horse with the pommels removed and the height adjusted. The height is set at 53 inches for vaults by men. It is lowered to a little over 49 inches for women.

The beatboard is a springboard device that helps to catapult you into the vault. Placed on the floor near the horse, it measures about 47 inches long, 24 inches wide, and 5 inches high. It is covered with a nonskid plastic material—about 1 inch thick—to protect the feet.

You'll likely see a variety of beatboards in your career as a gymnast. The most popular one in use today is the Reuther board, which was developed some years ago in Germany. It is the official board used in all top competitions.

In addition to the two basic pieces of equipment, there should be a thick mat placed on the far side of the horse for landings. A thinnish mat, usually measuring about ¾ inch thick, should be placed on the "runway"—the stretch of floor along which you must dash to the horse.

VAULTING COMPETITIONS

Vaulting has been a part of gymnastics competition since the late 1820s. Though open to both men and women, the two sexes are never pitted against each other. The same rule applies as in floor exercise: It's always the men against the men, and the women against the women.

There is one great difference between the two competitions. If you're a woman, you'll always vault across the width of the horse. If you are a man, your vaults will carry you above the length of the horse. For this reason, you'll often hear vaulting for men called the *long-horse* event.

In addition, there are two other less striking differences. First, a man must approach his vault with a run of no more than 65 feet, 7 inches. A woman is allowed a run of up to 78 feet. Both try to keep their runs well within the maximum distances, with the final length chosen depending on the individual.

The second has to do with the fact that the horse must be touched during a vault. A woman, flying across the width, will always touch the horse at its center. But for the man, the horse is divided into three sections; he may touch the horse on either end section, with his choice being determined by the vault being attempted. The center section may not be touched at any time. Even the slightest accidental touch will see the male gymnast's score lowered.

Once you get past these differences, the event is essentially the same for both sexes. No matter whether you're a man or a woman— and no matter how fundamental or advanced the vault may be— you're faced with the same problem. It's the problem of performing a stunt that has six parts to it. Each part must be correctly done if the vault is to be a success.

THE PARTS OF THE VAULT

The six parts are: (1) approach to the beatboard, (2) takeoff, (3) preflight, (4) contact with the horse, (5) postflight, and (6) landing.

Approach to the Beatboard: Your run to the beatboard starts with two or three trotting steps and then builds steadily until you're travel- ing just under full speed. Your greatest speed is attained about three or four strides before you reach the beatboard. Those final steps should all be of equal speed.

Run as if you're a sprinter, with your body slightly forward when you're moving the fastest. Pump your arms back and forth from the shoulders, keeping the arms bent and parallel to your sides; never let the arms swing over in front of your chest, a problem that troubles many women. Lengthen your strides as your speed increases.

Just what distance should you run? The answer will come only with experience. You'll need to experiment with several distances until you find that one that suits you best. Once it's found, stick with it and try to make all your approaches exactly the same—the same number of strides, the same length of stride, the same buildup of speed.

Though the beatboard is your target, you shouldn't stare at it dur- ing the run. You'll do better if, keeping in mind where you want to hit the board, you focus your gaze on both the board and the horse—plus some of the surrounding area. In this way, you'll have an overall pic- ture of where the vault is going to take you. As you near the end of the run, your focus should narrow itself to the horse.

The final step in the run is called the *hurdle*. It starts as a leaping action that sends your front foot off the floor. Follow immediately with the trailing foot and bring it forward so that the feet are together when you land on the beatboard. Don't allow yourself to land on just one foot, for then you'll skim across the horse in a low dive. Only with a feet-together landing will you be able to catapult to a height that will give your flight a look of beauty and permit you to touch the horse solidly as you pass.

The hurdle should be a continuation of the run, meaning that, without breaking stride, you should sail low through the air to the board. Just as you shouldn't permit yourself to land on one foot, neither should you allow yourself to hesitate and then jump onto the board with a hopping action. If you stay low, refusing to break stride, your forward speed will be easily converted into a rising movement when you catapult up from the board in the next instant.

Takeoff: The takeoff is the catapulting action that lifts you into the flight to the horse. For a good takeoff, end the hurdle by landing solidly on both feet at the point of maximum spring in the beatboard. This point is just to the rear of the highest spot in the arc of the board.

Your landing should be on the balls of the feet. Bend the hips, the knees, and the ankles slightly. Then quickly and forcefully straighten them, an action that will give you a strong thrust upward.

The arms also assist in the upward thrust. Many gymnasts have their own techniques for letting the arms help them. But it is suggested that you try the following method on your beginning vaults: just before stepping into the hurdle, swing your arms back and down. Then, on striking the board, whip them up and forward to shoulder level.

The position of the body when you hit the beatboard is important because your lean will determine the height to be reached in flying to the horse. If you lean forward, your flight will be low. If your body is vertical or leaning slightly backward, you'll fly higher.

The type of vault being attempted determines the height you'll need to achieve. As you become a more skillful gymnast, you'll be able to sail at whatever "altitude" is required. Most beginning vaults, however, call for you to land on the beatboard in a vertical position.

Preflight: This is the term for your flight to the horse. You should sail through the air with the body well extended and the arms held straight overhead. Your hands should be open and the palms down —ready to make contact with the horse.

Right from the start, develop the habit of getting as much loft and height as you can. Concentrate on not just skimming over the top of the horse. Remember, you need to touch the horse solidly as you pass. Then you'll be able to propel yourself high for the rest of the vault.

In time, you'll find that all sorts of technicalities surround the preflight. For instance, the angle of the body must never be less than twenty-five degrees above the horizontal surface of the horse. Also, the beatboard can be placed at various distances from the horse to produce certain kinds of preflights.

For instance, suppose you're a man planning to contact the horse at the *near end*—that's the end facing your line of approach; a low preflight is the best for this kind of vault, and it will be helped by placing the beatboard a goodly distance from the horse. But if you're heading for the *far end,* a higher preflight is needed. The beatboard should be moved closer to the horse.

But you'll learn all these technicalities as you go along. For now, as a beginner, concentrate on good loft, good height, and the good form that comes of holding your body well extended.

Contact with the horse: Contact is made with the hands—and with the hands only. They should be flat and shoulder distance apart, with the palms down at the end of straight arms. The fingers should always be aimed directly ahead.

Each entire hand touches the horse. Solidly. *But only for a split second.* Instantly, as if rebounding like two bouncing tennis balls, they push you up and over the horse. At the same time, there's an extra extension of the shoulders and the arms—and you're shot into the final phases of the vault.

Postflight: Also known as *afterflight,* this is the part of the vault that carries you from the horse and back to the floor. With a strong thrust upward from the horse, your postflight should be long and high

—somewhat higher, actually, than the preflight. Your back should be slightly arched as you sail through the air.

Landing: The landing here shares much in common with all other landings. Come down with legs together and meet the floor with the balls of your feet. As you drop, hold your arms in an extended position that you find comfortable and natural—perhaps out to the sides, perhaps forward and diagonally upward, perhaps straight overhead. Bend the knees on impact and then straighten them, drop the arms to your sides, and come to attention.

It's quite difficult to land without any excess movement because, unlike the landings in other events, you've no equipment nearby to hold for support. Your momentum always threatens you with a strong body waver or a stumble. You can help yourself to a steady landing by bringing your feet out a little ahead of your center of gravity as you descend. Experience will show you just how far they need to be brought forward.

From your very first practice session, concentrate on steady landings. Only with concentration and plenty of daily work will you be able to develop the body control necessary to avoid wavers and stumbles.

GETTING STARTED

Vaulting is not an event that demands or builds great strength, though the takeoff develops the legs, and the thrust at hand contact benefits the arms and shoulders. In the main, vaulting develops co-ordination, agility, and flexibility. And, as you advance from simple beginning flights to some very spectacular ones, it does wonders for your courage and daring.

You'll be wise if you come to the event with a good beginning background in tumbling. Then, before ever trying to sail across the horse, some time should be spent practicing, one at a time, the six parts of the vault. This can be done with a series of get-acquainted exercises.

Get-acquainted Exercises

There are many different get-acquainted exercises. Your coach will undoubtedly have some for you to try. And, before you're done, you'll likely be inventing several of your own. In the meantime, the following will give you the chance to work on each of the six parts in turn.

Approach, Hurdle, and Takeoff (Picture A): Place a beatboard in front of the floor mat. Concentrating on your form the whole time, run to the board, take off from both feet as if jumping over a low obstacle, and land on the pad. Later, place an obstacle between the board and the mat—perhaps a low bench or a rolled-up crash pad.

Preflight and Hand Contact (Pictures B, C, and D): Remember the *dive forward roll to a stand* in chapter 2? The action that opened it (Picture B) can be of value here. Dive forward to your hands for some preflight practice. But then do not roll forward as you did before. Rather, work on hand contact by instantly thrusting yourself back to a standing position. Included in the thrust should be a push of the hands and an extension of the shoulders and wrists.

For hand contact alone: Stand in front of a wall (Picture C), with arms extended directly ahead. Fall toward the wall, catch yourself with your hands, and instantly thrust yourself back straight again. Be sure to include the extension of the shoulders and the wrists along with the hand push.

For a fun way of practicing the hand thrust, get together with a friend for a game of "wheelbarrow." While your friend (Picture D) holds your ankles, keep pushing your hands clear of the floor with one upward thrust after another. After you've practiced a bit, try bounding up so energetically that there's time to clap your hands before returning them to the floor.

Postflight and Landing (Picture E): From a squat position on the horse, shoot yourself up straight and jump clear. Stretch your body out to its full length. Concentrate on keeping the legs together and on landing as steadily as you can. The jump is made from a squat rather than a standing position so that you can put full emphasis on stretching the body out straight. Also, you'll have the feeling of traveling a greater distance from start to finish.

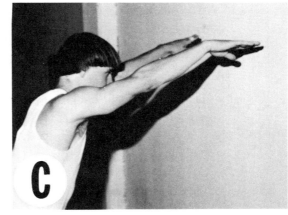

Vaulting: Get-acquainted Exercises

FIRST VAULTS

All beginners, regardless of whether they're men or women, first vault across the width of the horse. Later, after considerable practice, the men begin to work on the long horse. All the vaults that follow will carry you across the width. At the end of the chapter, there will be a section on those of their number that can then be attempted lengthwise.

We'll start with the most basic of all vaults.

Squat Vault

After placing the beatboard about two feet or so away from the horse, complete your approach run and takeoff. Extend the body in preflight (Picture A). But then, just as you're reaching the horse, lift the hips and tuck the legs. Bring your knees right against your chest (Picture B) as you carry yourself forward across the top of the horse by pushing down and back on your hands.

As your weight travels across the horse, push up and away (Picture C) with your hands. Hold the legs still deeply tucked as you fly away. Then, in the instant when you know that you're safely clear of the horse (Picture D), snap your body open, extending it fully and stretching your arms overhead. Drop to a landing (Picture E) on the balls of your feet.

The vault should be learned a step at a time. Concentrate first on passing through the squat position; move the beatboard right up to the horse, forget about the preflight, and put your hands on the horse as soon as you take off. Let your hands carry you upward while you tuck the legs deeply. And let your feet land on the horse. Pause for a moment, getting the feel of the squat position, and then thrust into the postflight. After you've got these actions down pat, add the preflight, still stopping for a moment with your feet on the horse. Finally, it will be time to travel nonstop through the entire vault.

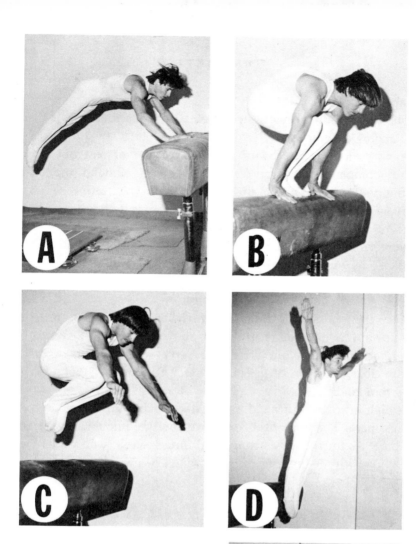

The Squat Vault

Stoop Vault

The stoop vault is much the same as its squat cousin. But there's a challenging difference. . . .

Again, with the beatboard placed a couple of feet out from the horse, complete your approach and takeoff. Extend the body in preflight (Picture A), but lift the hips high by starting to pike the body as you sail forward. The hips should be well above your head by the time your hands touch the horse.

Now comes the action that makes this vault different and more challenging. As you make hand contact (Picture B), complete the body pike and whip the legs downward. But don't bend them into a tuck.

Keep them perfectly straight. In the instant of the pike, thrust yourself upward. While you're in the air above the horse (Picture C), the legs shoot between your arms and carry you forward. As soon as you're clear, snap out of the pike, stretch full length (Picture D), and drop to a landing.

A high lift of the hips and a very strong hand thrust are the keys to success here. The lift is needed to give you the time and the height for the pike. As for the very strong hand thrust—well, who wants the feet to collide with the horse as the legs swing downward?

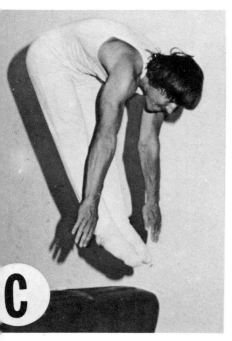

The Stoop Vault

Straddle Vault

The straddle vault adds another degree of challenge. It's performed in the same way as the stoop vault, but with a lift of the hips that isn't quite so high. Then—with the picture telling all—the legs come forward in the straddle position. They remain to the outside of the arms until you're clear of the horse and are able to straighten for the landing.

Like the stoop vault, the straddle can be learned a step at a time. To acquaint yourself with the position try it on the floor, supporting yourself on your hands. Then end each preflight by sitting on the horse for a moment before thrusting away.

The Straddle Vault

The Flank Vault

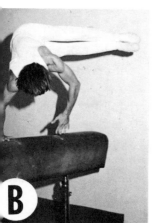

Flank Vault

Still another degree of challenge—this time a sideways turn of the body and the use of just one arm in the thrust to postflight.

In preflight (Picture A), the hips are raised, the legs are gently piked, and the hands are extended to the horse. In the instant that you touch the horse, pike the legs sharply and send them out to the side and upward (Picture B), turning one hip down toward the horse. In this instance, the legs are being swung to the left, but they may be aimed in the opposite direction just as easily.

Carry the legs forward until they're passing above the horse. At that moment (Picture C), raise the left hand high. Supporting yourself on the right arm only, straighten from the pike, arch your back slightly, and thrust into a postflight that will see you turn yourself so that you land (Picture D) with your back to the horse.

It's best to learn the flank vault in stages. Start by swinging the legs sideways to the horse, letting them rest for an instant, and then thrusting off into the postflight. Next, hold the pike position all the way to the postflight, concentrating on raising the left arm and supporting yourself on the right. Then begin to experiment with straightening the legs at the appropriate moment.

LONG-HORSE VAULTING

With the exception of the flank, all the above vaults can be transferred to the long horse. They may be performed with preflights to the near end or to the far end.

All long-horse vaults are exciting stunts, requiring strong approaches and preflights, and very vigorous thrusts into postflight. Exciting though they promise to be, please don't let your eagerness to try them get the better of you. They demand more than a beginning skill and so should be saved for the proper moment. The wait will be more than worthwhile. You'll save yourself many an unnecessary bruise and will have the pleasure of perfecting each vault more quickly.

10   A Look to the Future

QUESTION: Just what does the future hold for you in gymnastics?
ANSWER: Some of the most exciting work you've ever done.

The next pages will show you just how exciting. Each is given to an intermediate or advanced stunt from one of the competitive events. All eight events are represented. The stunts have been picked on the basis of their known popularity with gymnasts.

Let's take a look. (*overleaf*)

*   *   *

FLOOR EXERCISE

The Layout Back Somersault

The layout back somersault is a somersault performed with the body straight or slightly arched, and the one pictured has long been a favorite with both men and women gymnasts. With the body fully extended and rotating like the spokes in a wheel, it sends you high above the gymnasium floor.

The somersault begins with a vertical leap from both feet after you've gained momentum with a run and a handspring or some other similar movement. Instantly, extending the body fully, carry yourself along an arcing path upward and to the rear. Smoothly, gracefully, your body rotates as you rise until, at the height of the somersault, you're poised upside down in the air, with your legs aimed at the ceiling.

The rotating action continues. Down the far side of the arc you travel, at last dropping feet first to a landing on bent knees. Top gymnasts are able to land on just one foot.

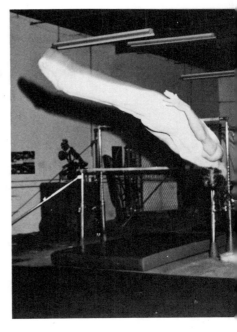

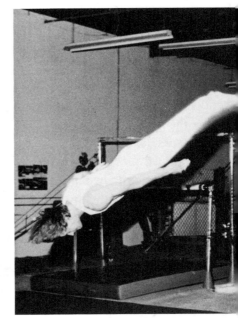

The Layout Back Somersault

Just how high does the somersault carry you? It depends on how tall you are. You should be lifted above head height.

THE BALANCE BEAM

The Split

One of the most demanding movements in gymnastics, the split is used on the balance beam and in floor exercise. It requires great flexibility, muscle control, and balance.

Pictured is the *front split*. To begin, stand facing the length of the beam, with one leg slightly ahead of the other. Then, smoothly and steadily, slide the front leg forward and the rear leg backward until you've descended to the full split position. On reaching the full split, your front knee should be turned upward, and your rear knee downward.

The Front Split

Throughout the movement, your arms and hands may be held in any position that is comfortable and graceful.

The split may also be performed laterally—that is, with the body and head facing to the side. The lateral split ends with both knees turned upward.

You can start to practice the split while you're still a beginner. Work slowly, though. Lower yourself by degrees over a period of days or weeks. Your muscles will need time to grow flexible enough for the movement.

THE UNEVEN PARALLEL BARS

The Hecht

The hecht is one of the most breathtaking ways to dismount the uneven bars. It begins as you swing forward from the high bar and strike the low bar. Piking the body sharply and releasing the high bar, you circle beneath the low bar and rise to the top. As you approach the top, you "pop" your body open forcefully and push your hips hard against the bar.

This forceful "pop," combined with the hip push, lifts you clear of the bar and carries you forward in a swan dive. Once clear of the bar, your legs head floorward and you drop to a landing.

The hecht may also be performed on the high bar. Cast out from the bar, then come forward to whip around it, pop the body open, and sail outward for the landing.

If you wish, you may perform the hecht on the high bar or on the low bar with the legs straddled. But the dismount is considered more difficult when done with the legs together, and so will earn you a higher score. Accomplished gymnasts are able to add a half or a full twist of the body as they leave the bar and head for the floor.

The Hecht

THE RINGS

The Cross

Here's the hold position that, as any ring man will tell you, requires just about the greatest strength in all gymnastics. With the arms extended straight out to the sides and the body absolutely vertical, the position must be held motionless for at least two seconds.

They can be two very long seconds—indeed!

The cross was originally known as the iron cross.

The Cross

THE SIDE HORSE

The Flank Circle

As a beginner, you practiced single-leg circles in chapter 6. By the time you reach advanced gymnastics, you'll be working on some very challenging double-leg movements. Right at the top of the list will be the flank circle.

Starting with a feint on the right pommel and then supporting yourself on one arm, swing the legs along the rear of the horse and carry them across the left end. Then down the front of the horse they move to rise above the right end and complete the circle.

Keep the legs straight and together, with the toes pointed, throughout the circle. Grip both pommels as the legs sweep along the front of the horse. Then clear a path by pulling up the right hand as you flow across the right end to finish the movement.

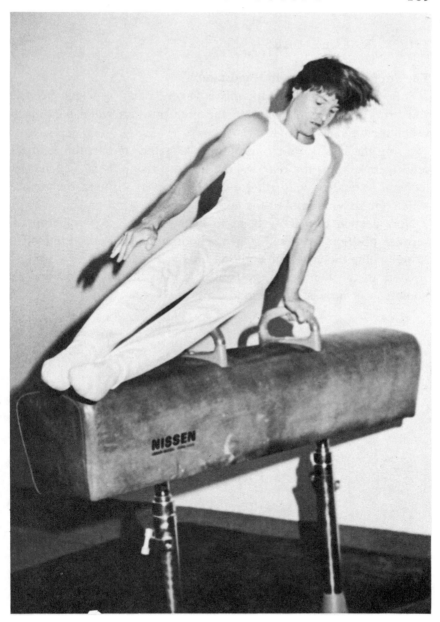

The Flank Circle

THE PARALLEL BARS

The Straight-body Press to Handstand

Solid strength is a must for this advanced balance, which begins as you bring your legs forward to the pike position while hanging between the bars in a straight-arm support.

Swing the legs down from the pike to gather momentum and then send them high to the rear. As the legs are rising, bend your elbows, let your extended body tilt forward, and pass through the point at which you're horizontal to the floor.

Now deepen the elbow bend to help send the legs right up to a vertical position overhead. Then smoothly finish everything off by straightening the arms and entering the handstand.

Once in the handstand, you must remain there—poised and motionless—for at least two seconds.

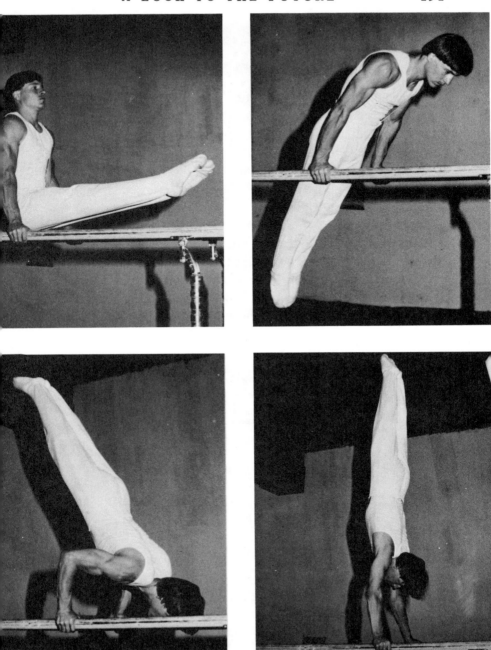

The Straight-body Press to Handstand

THE HORIZONTAL BAR

The Stemme

This is the movement most often used by accomplished gymnasts to begin their competitive routines. It's a very quick and efficient way of "climbing" to a high position from which some very breathtaking swings can be launched.

Jump straight up and catch the bar in the reverse grip. A pendulum swing, combined with a strong pull of the arms, lifts you until your shoulders are above the bar.

Piking the body, swing down beneath the bar and send your legs up the far side. Follow them right up, with your hands pushing and your arms straightening until you reach the handstand position.

And there you are—at the very top of the movement.

But the handstand mustn't be held. Remember, there may be no stops or even hesitations on the horizontal bar. And so don't let a breath go by before launching into your first swing.

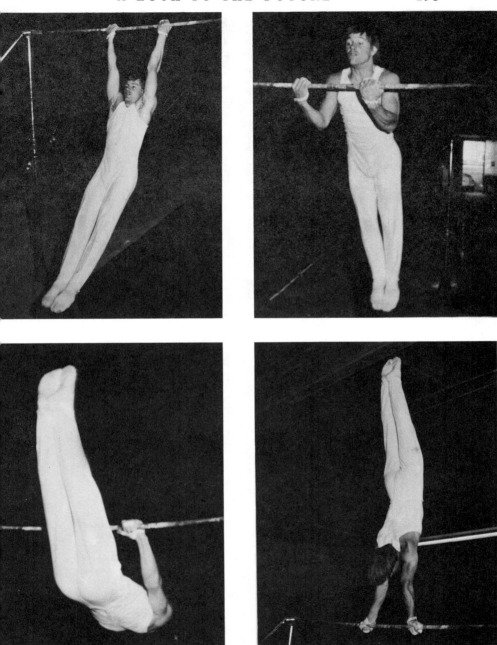

The Stemme

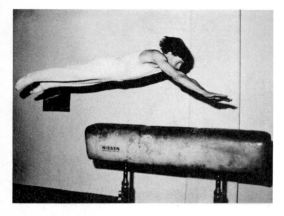 

The Long-horse Straddle Vault

VAULTING

The Long-horse Straddle Vault

Here's the straddle vault performed along the length of the horse. The pictures tell all, showing first the strong preflight that's needed to carry you to the far end, and then the energetic lift that catapults you into the postflight.

A FINAL NOTE

As you're working to become an expert gymnast, you may want to read more about your sport. Among the many books that you'll find in your public library, the following should prove to be especially helpful:

Inside Gymnastics by Ed Gagnier (Henry Regnery Company, Chicago), *Gymnastics for Men* by Eric Hughes (Ronald Press Company, New York), *Olympic Gymnastics* by Akitomo Kaneko (Sterling Publishing Company, New York), *Complete Book of Gymnastics* by Newton C. Loken and Robert J. Willoughby (Prentice-Hall, Inc., Englewood Cliffs, New Jersey), *Gymnastics and You* by Michael Resnick (Rand McNally & Company, Skokie, Illinois), and *Gymnastics for Women* by Andrea Bodo Schmid and Blanche Jessen Drury (Mayfield Publishing Company, Palo Alto, California).

AUTHOR BIOGRAPHY

EDWARD F. DOLAN, JR., was born and educated in California, and has lived in that state for most of his life. After serving in the 101st Airborne Division during World War II, he spent seven years as a free-lance writer in radio and television, and was a teacher for some years after that. His first book was published in 1958. Since then, he has written more than thirty-five books for young people and adults. He and his wife, Rose, live just north of San Francisco.

Index